Foreign Travelers in America
1810–1935

Foreign Travelers in America
1810–1935

Advisory Editors:

Arthur M. Schlesinger, Jr.
Eugene P. Moehring

THE
FUTURE IN AMERICA

H. G. WELLS

ARNO PRESS
A New York Times Company
New York—1974

Reprint Edition 1974 by Arno Press Inc.

Copyright © 1906 by Harper & Brothers
Reprinted by permission of The Estate
  of the late H. G. Wells

Reprinted from a copy in
  The University of Illinois Library

TRAVELERS IN AMERICA, 1810-1935
ISBN for complete set: 0-405-05440-8
See last pages of this volume for titles.

Manufactured in the United States of America

Library of Congress Cataloging in Publication Data

Wells, Herbert George, 1866-1946.
   The future in America.

   (Foreign travelers in America, 1810-1935)
   Reprint of the ed. published by Harper, New York.
   1. National characteristics, American. 2. United
States--Social conditions--1865-1918. I. Title.
II. Series.
E169.1.W35 1974   917.3'03'91   73-13156
ISBN 0-405-05469-6

THE
FUTURE IN AMERICA

FIFTH AVENUE, NEW YORK

THE
FUTURE IN AMERICA

A SEARCH AFTER REALITIES

BY

H. G. WELLS

AUTHOR OF
"ANTICIPATIONS" "THE WAR OF THE WORLDS"
"THIRTY STRANGE STORIES" ETC.

ILLUSTRATED

HARPER & BROTHERS PUBLISHERS
NEW YORK AND LONDON

CONTENTS

ILLUSTRATIONS

THE FUTURE IN AMERICA

THE FUTURE IN AMERICA

CHAPTER I

THE PROPHETIC HABIT OF MIND

(At a writing-desk in Sandgate)

I

"ARE you a Polygamist?"

The Question   "Are you an Anarchist?"

The questions seem impertinent. They are part of a long paper of interrogations I must answer satisfactorily if I am to be regarded as a desirable alien to enter the United States of America. I want very much to pass that great statue of Liberty illuminating the World (from a central position in New York Harbor), in order to see things in its light, to talk to certain people, to appreciate certain atmospheres, and so I resist the provocation to answer impertinently. I do not even volunteer that I do not smoke and am a total abstainer; on which points it would seem the States as a whole still keep an open mind. I am full of curiosity about America, I am possessed by a prob-

I

lem I feel I cannot adequately discuss even with myself except over there, and I must go even at the price of coming to a decision upon the theoretically open questions these two inquiries raise.

My problem I know will seem ridiculous and monstrous when I give it in all its stark disproportions—attacked by me with my equipment it will call up an image of an elephant assailed by an ant who has not even mastered Jiu-jitsu—but at any rate I've come to it in a natural sort of way and it is one I must, for my own peace of mind, make some kind of attempt upon, even if at last it means no more than the ant crawling in an exploratory way hither and thither over that vast unconscious carcass and finally getting down and going away. That may be rather good for the ant, and the experience may be of interest to other ants, however infinitesimal from the point of view of the elephant, the final value of his investigation may be. And this tremendous problem in my case and now in this—simply; What is going to happen to the United States of America in the next thirty years or so?

I do not know if the reader has ever happened upon any books or writings of mine before, but if, what is highly probable, he has not, he may be curious to know how it is that any human being should be running about in so colossally an interrogative state of mind. (For even the present inquiry is by no means my maximum limit). And the ex-

2

planation is to be found a little in a mental idiosyncrasy perhaps, but much more in the development of a special way of thinking, of a habit of mind.

That habit of mind may be indicated by a proposition that, with a fine air of discovery, I threw out some years ago, in a happy ignorance that I had been anticipated by no less a person than Heraclitus. "There is no Being but Becoming," that was what appeared to my unscholarly mind to be almost triumphantly new. I have since then informed myself more fully about Heraclitus, there are moments now when I more than half suspect that all the thinking I shall ever do will simply serve to illuminate my understanding of him, but at any rate that apothegm of his does exactly convey the intellectual attitude into which I fall. I am curiously not interested in things, and curiously interested in the consequences of things. I wouldn't for the world go to see the United States for what they are—if I had sound reason for supposing that the entire western hemisphere was to be destroyed next Christmas, I should not, I think, be among the multitude that would rush for one last look at that great spectacle,—from which it follows naturally that I don't propose to see Niagara. I should much more probably turn an inquiring visage eastward, with the west so certainly provided for. I have come to be, I am afraid, even a little insensitive to fine immediate things through this anticipatory habit.

This habit of mind confronts and perplexes my sense of things that simply *are*, with my brooding preoccupation with how they will shape presently, what they will lead to, what seed they will sow and how they will wear. At times, I can assure the reader, this quality approaches otherworldliness, in its constant reference to an all-important hereafter. There are times indeed when it makes life seem so transparent and flimsy, seem so dissolving, so passing on to an equally transitory series of consequences, that the enhanced sense of instability becomes restlessness and distress; but on the other hand nothing that exists, nothing whatever, remains altogether vulgar or dull and dead or hopeless in its light. But the interest is shifted. The pomp and splendor of established order, the braying triumphs, ceremonies, consummations, one sees these glittering shows for what they are—through their threadbare grandeur shine the little significant things that will make the future. . . .

And now that I am associating myself with great names, let me discover that I find this characteristic turn of mind of mine, not only in Heraclitus, the most fragmentary of philosophers, but for one fine passage at any rate, in Mr. Henry James, the least fragmentary of novelists. In his recent impressions of America I find him apostrophizing the great mansions of Fifth Avenue, in words quite after my heart;—

"It's all very well," he writes, "for you to look

4

as if, since you've had no past, you're going in, as
the next best thing, for a magnificent compensatory
future. What are you going to make your future
of, for all your airs, we want to know? What elements of a future, as futures have gone in the great
world, are at all assured to you?"

I had already when I read that, figured myself
as addressing if not these particular last triumphs
of the fine Transatlantic art of architecture, then
at least America in general in some such words. It
is not unpleasant to be anticipated by the chief
Master of one's craft, it is indeed, when one reflects
upon his peculiar intimacy with this problem, enormously reassuring, and so I have very gladly annexed his phrasing and put it here to honor and
adorn and in a manner to explain my own enterprise. I have already studied some of these fine
buildings through the mediation of an illustrated
magazine—they appear solid, they appear wonderful and well done to the highest pitch—and before
many days now I shall, I hope, reconstruct that
particular moment, stand—the latest admirer from
England—regarding these portentous magnificences,
from the same sidewalk—will they call it?—as my
illustrious predecessor, and with his question ringing in my mind all the louder for their proximity,
and the universally acknowledged invigoration of
the American atmosphere. "What are you going
to make your future *of*, for all your airs?"

And then I suppose I shall return to crane my

neck at the Flat-Iron Building or the *Times* sky-scraper, and ask all that too, an identical question.

II

CERTAIN phases in the development
Philosophical of these prophetic exercises one may
perhaps be permitted to trace.

To begin with, I remember that to me in my boy-hood speculation about the Future was a monstrous joke. Like most people of my generation I was launched into life with millennial assumptions. This present sort of thing, I believed, was going on for a time, interesting personally perhaps but as a whole inconsecutive, and then—it might be in my lifetime or a little after it—there would be trumpets and shoutings and celestial phenomena, a battle of Armageddon and the Judgment. As I saw it, it was to be a strictly protestant and individualistic judgment, each soul upon its personal merits. To talk about the Man of the Year Million was of course in the face of this great conviction, a whimsical play of fancy. The Year Million was just as im-possible, just as gayly nonsensical as fairy-land. . . .

I was a student of biology before I realized that this, my finite and conclusive End, at least in the material and chronological form, had somehow vanished from the scheme of things. In the place of it had come a blackness and a vagueness about

the endless vista of years ahead, that was tremendous—that terrified. That is a phase in which lots
of educated people remain to this day. "All this
scheme of things, life, force, destiny which began not
six thousand years, mark you, but an infinity ago,
that has developed out of such strange weird shapes
and incredible first intentions, out of gaseous nebulæ,
carboniferous swamps, saurian giantry and arboreal
apes, is by the same tokens to continue, developing
—into what?" That was the overwhelming riddle
that came to me, with that realization of an End
averted, that has come now to most of our world.

The phase that followed the first helpless stare of
the mind was a wild effort to express one's sudden
apprehension of unlimited possibility. One made
fantastic exaggerations, fantastic inversions of all
recognized things. Anything of this sort might
come, anything of any sort. The books about the
future that followed the first stimulus of the world's
realization of the implications of Darwinian science,
have all something of the monstrous experimental
imaginings of children. I myself, in my microcos-
mic way, duplicated the times. Almost the first
thing I ever wrote—it survives in an altered form
as one of a bookful of essays,—was of this type;
"The Man of the Year Million," was presented as a
sort of pantomime head and a shrivelled body, and
years after that, the *Time Machine*, my first published book, ran in the same vein. At that point,
at a brief astonished stare down the vistas of time-

to-come, at something between wonder and amazed,. incredulous, defeated laughter, most people, I think, stop. But those who are doomed to the prophetic habit of mind go on.

The next phase, the third phase, is to shorten the range of the outlook, to attempt something a little more proximate than the final destiny of man. One becomes more systematic, one sets to work to trace the great changes of the last century or so, and one produces these in a straight line and according to the rule of three. If the maximum velocity of land travel in 1800 was twelve miles an hour and in 1900 (let us say) sixty miles an hour, then one concludes that in 2000 A.D. it will be three hundred miles an hour. If the population of America in 1800— but I refrain from this second instance. In that fashion one got out a sort of gigantesque caricature of the existing world, everything swollen to vast proportions and massive beyond measure. In my case that phase produced a book, *When the Sleeper Wakes*, in which, I am told, by competent New-Yorkers, that I, starting with London, an unbiassed mind, this rule-of-three method and my otherwise unaided imagination, produced something more like Chicago than any other place wherein righteous men are likely to be found. That I shall verify in due course, but my present point is merely that to write such a book is to discover how thoroughly wrong this all too obvious method of enlarging the present is.

THE PROPHETIC HABIT OF MIND

One goes on therefore—if one is to succumb altogether to the prophetic habit—to a really "scientific" attack upon the future. The "scientific" phase is not final, but it is far more abundantly fruitful than its predecessors. One attempts a rude wide analysis of contemporary history, one seeks to clear and detach operating causes and to work them out, and so, combining this necessary set of consequences with that, to achieve a synthetic forecast in terms just as broad and general and vague as the causes considered are few. I made, it happens, an experiment in this scientific sort of prophecy in a book called *Anticipations*, and I gave an altogether excessive exposition and defence of it, I went altogether too far in this direction, in a lecture to the Royal Institution, "The Discovery of the Future," that survives in odd corners as a pamphlet, and is to be found, like a scrap of old newspaper in the roof gutter of a museum, in *Nature* (vol. LXV., p. 326) and in the Smithsonian Report (for 1902). Within certain limits, however, I still believe this scientific method is sound. It gives sound results in many cases, results at any rate as sound as those one gets from the "laws" of political economy; one can claim it really does effect a sort of prophecy on the material side of life.

For example, it was quite obvious about 1899 that invention and enterprise were very busy with the means of locomotion, and one could deduce from that certain practically inevitable consequences

9

in the distribution of urban populations. With easier, quicker means of getting about there were endless reasons, hygienic, social, economic, why people should move from the town centres towards their peripheries, and very few why they should not. The towns one inferred therefore, would get slacker, more diffused, the country-side more urban. From that, from the spatial widening of personal interests that ensued, one could infer certain changes in the spirits of local politics, and so one went on to a number of fairly valid adumbrations. Then again starting from the practical supersession in the long run of all unskilled labor by machinery one can work out with a pretty fair certainty many coming social developments, and the broad trend of one group of influences at least from the moral attitude of the mass of common people. In industry, in domestic life again, one foresees a steady development of complex appliances, demanding, and indeed in an epoch of frequently changing methods *forcing*, a flexible understanding, versatility of effort, a universal rising standard of education. So too a study of military methods and apparatus convinces one of the necessary transfer of power in the coming century from the ignorant and enthusiastic masses who made the revolutions of the eighteenth and nineteenth centuries and won Napoleon his wars, to any more deliberate, more intelligent and more disciplined class that may possess an organized purpose. But where will one find that class? There comes a question that goes outside science, that takes one at once into a field beyond the range of the "scientific" method altogether.

So long as one adopts the assumptions of the old political economist and assumes men without idiosyncrasy, without prejudices, without, as people say, wills of their own, so long as one imagines a perfectly acquiescent humanity that will always in the long run under pressure liquefy and stream along the line of least resistance to its own material advantage, the business of prophecy is easy. But from the first I felt distrust for that facility in prophesying, I perceived that always there lurked something, an incalculable opposition to these mechanically conceived forces, in law, in usage and prejudice, in the poïetic power of exceptional individual men. I discovered for myself over again, the inseparable nature of the two functions of the prophet. In my *Anticipations*, for example, I had intended simply to work out and foretell, and before I had finished I was in a fine full blast of exhortation. . . .

That by an easy transition brought me to the last stage in the life history of the prophetic mind, as it is at present known to me. One comes out on the other side of the "scientific" method, into the large temperance, the valiant inconclusiveness, the released creativeness of philosophy. Much may be foretold as certain, much more as possible, but the last decisions and the greatest decisions, lie in the hearts and wills of unique incalculable men. With them we have to deal as our ultimate reality in all these matters, and our methods have to be not "scientific" at all for all the greater issues, the humanly important issues, but critical, literary, even if you will—artistic. Here insight is of more account than induction and the perception of fine tones than the counting of heads. Science deals with necessity and necessity is here but the firm ground on which our freedom goes. One passes from affairs of predestination to affairs of free will.

This discovery spread at once beyond the field of prophesying. The end, the aim, the test of science, as a model man understands the word, is foretelling by means of "laws," and my error in attempting a complete "scientific" forecast of human affairs arose in too careless an assent to the ideas about me, and from accepting uncritically such claims as that history should be "scientific," and that economics and sociology (for example) are "sciences." Directly one gauges the fuller implications of that uniqueness of individuals Darwin's work has so permanently illuminated, one passes beyond that. The ripened prophet realizes Schopenhauer—as indeed I find Professor Munsterberg saying. "The deepest sense of human affairs is reached," he writes, "when we consider them not as appearances but as decisions." There one has the same thing coming to meet one from the psychological side. . . .

But my present business isn't to go into this shadowy, metaphysical foundation world on which our thinking rests, but to the brightly lit overworld of America. This philosophical excursion is set here just to prepare the reader quite frankly for speculations and to disabuse his mind of the idea that in writing of the Future in America I'm going to write of houses a hundred stories high and flying-machines in warfare and things like that. I am not going to America to work a pretentious horo-scope, to discover a Destiny, but to find out what I can of what must needs make that Destiny,—a great nation's Will.

III

THE material factors in a nation's
The Will of future are subordinate factors, they
America present advantages, such as the easy access of the English to coal and the sea, or dis-advantages, such as the ice-bound seaboard of the Russians, but these are the circumstances and not necessarily the rulers of its fate. The essential factor in the destiny of a nation, as of a man and of mankind, lies in the form of its will and in the quality and quantity of its will. The drama of a nation's future, as of a man's, lies in this conflict of its will with what would else be "scientifically" predictable, materially inevitable. If the man, if the nation was an automaton fitted with good

average motives, so and so, one could say exactly, would be done. It's just where the thing isn't automatic that our present interest comes in.

I might perhaps reverse the order of the three aspects of will I have named, for manifestly where the quantity of will is small, it matters nothing what the form or quality. The man or the people that wills feebly is the sport of every circumstance, and there if anywhere the scientific method holds truest or even altogether true. Do geographical positions or mineral resources make for riches? Then such a people will grow insecurely and disastrously rich. Is an abundant prolific life at a low level indicated? They will pullulate and suffer. If circumstances make for a choice between comfort and reproduction, your feeble people will dwindle and pass; if war, if conquest tempt them then they will turn from all preoccupations and follow the drums. Little things provoke their unstable equilibrium, to hostility, to forgiveness. . . .

And be it noted that the quantity of will in a nation is not necessarily determined by adding up the wills of all its people. I am told, and I am disposed to believe it, that the Americans of the United States are a people of great individual force of will, the clear strong faces of many young Americans, something almost Roman in the faces of their statesmen and politicians, a distinctive quality I detect in such Americans as I have met, a quality of sharply cut determination even though it be only about details and secondary things, that one must rouse one's self to meet, inclines me to give a provisional credit to that, but how far does all this possible will-force aggregate to a great national purpose?—what algebraically does it add up to when this and that have cancelled each other? That may be a different thing altogether.

And next to this net quantity of will a nation or people may possess, come the questions of its quality, its flexibility, its consciousness and intellectuality. A nation may be full of will and yet inflexibly and disastrously stupid in the expression of that will. There was probably more will-power, more haughty and determined self-assertion in the young bull that charged the railway engine than in several regiments of men, but it was after all a low quality of will with no method but a violent and injudicious directness, and in the end it was suicidal and futile. There again is the substance for ramifying Enquiries. How subtle, how collected and patient, how far capable of a long plan, is this American nation? Suppose it has a will so powerful and with such resources that whatever simple end may be attained by rushing upon it is America's for the asking, there still remains the far more important question of the ends that are not obvious, that are intricate and complex and not to be won by booms and cataclysms of effort.

An Englishman comes to think that most of the permanent and precious things for which a nation's effort goes are like that, and here too I have an open mind and unsatisfied curiosities.

And lastly there is the form of the nation's purpose. I have been reading what I can find about that in books for some time, and now I want to cross over the Atlantic, more particularly for that, to question more or less openly certain Americans, not only men and women, but the mute expressive presences of house and appliance, of statue, flag and public building, and the large collective visages of crowds, what it is all up to, what it thinks it is all after, how far it means to escape or improve upon its purely material destinies? I want over there to find whatever consciousness or vague consciousness of a common purpose there may be, what is their Vision, their American Utopia, how much will there is shaping to attain it, how much capacity goes with the will—what, in short, there is in America, over and above the mere mechanical consequences of scattering multitudes of energetic Europeans athwart a vast healthy, productive and practically empty continent in the temperate zone. There you have the terms of reference of an enquiry, that is I admit (as Mr. Morgan Richards the eminent advertisement agent would say), "mammoth in character."

The American reader may very reasonably inquire at this point why an Englishman does not begin with the future of his own country. The answer is that this particular one has done so, and that in many ways he has found his intimacy and proximity a disadvantage. One knows too much of the things that seem to matter and that ultimately don't, one is full of misleading individual instances intensely seen, one can't see the wood for the trees. One comes to America at last, not only with the idea of seeing America, but with something more than an incidental hope of getting one's own England there in the distance and as a whole, for the first time in one's life. And the problem of America, from this side anyhow, has an air of being simpler. For all the Philippine adventure her future still seems to lie on the whole compactly in one continent, and not as ours is, dispersed round and about the habitable globe, strangely entangled with India, with Japan, with Africa and with the great antagonism the Germans force upon us at our doors. Moreover one cannot look ten years ahead in England, without glancing across the Atlantic. "There they are," we say to one another, "those Americans! They speak our language, read our books, give us books, share our mind. What we think still goes into their heads in a measure, and their thoughts run through our brains. What will they be up to?"

Our future is extraordinarily bound up in America's and in a sense dependent upon it. It is not that we dream very much of political reunions of Anglo Saxondom and the like. So long as we British retain our wide and accidental sprawl of empire about the earth we cannot expect or desire the Americans to share our stresses and entanglements. Our Empire has its own adventurous and perilous outlook. But our civilization is a different thing from our Empire, a thing that reaches out further into the future, that will be going on changed beyond recognition. Because of our common language, of our common traditions, Americans are a part of our community, are becoming indeed the larger part of our community of thought and feeling and outlook—in a sense far more intimate than any link we have with Hindoo or Copt or Cingalese. A common Englishman has an almost pathetic pride and sense of proprietorship in the States; he is fatally ready to fall in with the idea that two nations that share their past, that still, a little restively, share one language, may even contrive to share an infinitely more interesting future. Even if he does not chance to be an American now, his grandson may be. America is his inheritance, his reserved accumulating investment. In that sense indeed America belongs to the whole western world; all Europe owns her promise, but to the Englishman the sense of participation is intense. "*We* did it," he will tell of the most American of achievements, of the settlement of the middle west for example, and this is so far justifiable that numberless men, myself included, are Englishmen, Australian, New-Zealand-ers, Canadians, instead of being Americans, by the merest accidents of life. My father still possesses the stout oak box he had had made to emigrate withal, everything was arranged that would have got me and my brothers born across the ocean, and only the coincidence of a business opportunity and an illness of my mother's, arrested that. It was so near a thing as that with me, which prevents my blood from boiling with patriotic indignation instead of patriotic solicitude at the frequent sight of red-coats as I see them from my study window going to and fro to Shorncliffe camp.

Well I learn from Professor Münsterberg how vain my sense of proprietorship is, but still this much of it obstinately remains, that I will at any rate *look* at the American future.

By the accidents that delayed that box it comes about that if I want to see what America is up to, I have among other things to buy a Baedeker and a steamer ticket and fill up the inquiring blanks in this remarkable document before me, the long string of questions that begins:—

"Are you a Polygamist?"

"Are you an Anarchist?"

Here I gather is one little indication of the great will I am going to study. It would seem that the United States of America regard Anarchy and Polygamy with aversion, regard indeed Anarchists and Polygamists as creatures unfit to mingle with the already very various eighty million of citizens who constitute their sovereign powers, and on the other hand hold these creatures so inflexibly honorable as certainly to tell these damning truths about themselves in this matter. . . .

It's a little odd. One has a second or so of doubt about the quality of that particular manifestation of will.

CHAPTER II

MATERIAL PROGRESS
(On the "Carmania" going Americanward)

I

American
Certitudes WHEN one talks to an American of his national purpose he seems a little at a loss; if one speaks of his national destiny, he responds with alacrity. I make this generalization on the usual narrow foundations, but so the impression comes to me.

Until this present generation, indeed until within a couple of decades, it is not very evident that Americans did envisage any national purpose at all, except in so far as there was a certain solicitude not to be cheated out of an assured destiny. A sort of optimistic fatalism possessed them. They had, and mostly it seems they still have, a tremendous sense of sustained and assured growth, and it is not altogether untrue that one is told—I have been told—such things as that "America is a great country, sir," that its future is gigantic and that it is already (and going to be more and more so) the greatest country on earth.

THE FUTURE IN AMERICA

I am not the sort of Englishman who questions that. I do so regard that much as obvious and true that it seems to me even a little undignified, as well as a little overbearing, for Americans to insist upon it so; I try to go on as soon as possible to the question just how my interlocutor *shapes* that gigantic future and what that world predominance is finally to do for us in England and all about the world. So far, I must insist, I haven't found anything like an idea. I have looked for it in books, in papers, in speeches and now I am going to look for it in America. At the most I have found vague imaginings that correspond to that first or monstrous stage in the scheme of prophetic development I sketched in my opening.

There is often no more than a volley of rhetorical blank-cartridge. So empty is it of all but sound that I have usually been constrained by civility from going on to a third enquiry;—

"And what are you, sir, doing in particular, to assist and enrich this magnificent and quite indefinable Destiny of which you so evidently feel yourself a part?" . . .

That seems to be really no unjust rendering of the conscious element of the American outlook as one finds it, for example, in these nice-looking and pleasant-mannered fellow-passengers upon the *Carmania* upon whom I fasten with leading questions and experimental remarks. One exception I discover—a pleasant New York clubman who has doubts of this and that. The discipline and sense of purpose in Germany has laid hold upon him. He seems to be, in contrast with his fellow-countrymen, almost pessimistically aware that the American ship of state is after all a mortal ship and liable to leakages. There are certain problems and dangers he seems to think that may delay, perhaps even prevent, an undamaged arrival in that predestined port, that port too resplendent for the eye to rest upon; a Chinese peril, he thinks has not been finally dealt with, "race suicide" is not arrested for all that it is scolded in a most valiant and virile manner, and there are adverse possibilities in the immigrant, in the black, the socialist, against which he sees no guarantee. He sees huge danger in the development and organization of the new finance and no clear promise of a remedy. He finds the closest parallel between the American Republic and Rome before the coming of Imperialism. But these other Americans have no share in his pessimisms. They may confess to as much as he does in the way of dangers, admit there are occasions for calking, a need of stopping quite a number of possibilities if the American Idea is to make its triumphant entry at last into that port of blinding accomplishment, but, apart from a few necessary preventive proposals, I do not perceive any extensive sense of anything whatever to be done, anything to be shaped and thought out and made in the sense of a national determination to a designed and specified end.

II

THERE are, one must admit, tremen-
A Symbol of Progress dous justifications for the belief in a
sort of automatic ascent of American
things to unprecedented magnificences, an ascent
so automatic that indeed one needn't bother in the
slightest to keep the whole thing going. For example, consider this, last year's last-word in ocean
travel in which I am crossing, the *Carmania* with
its unparalleled steadfastness, its racing, tireless
great turbines, its vast population of 3244 souls!
It has on the whole a tremendous effect of having
come by fate and its own forces. One forgets that
any one planned it, much of it indeed has so much
the quality of moving, as the planets move, in the
very nature of things. You go aft and see the
wake tailing away across the blue ridges, you go forward and see the cleft water, lift protestingly, roll
back in an indignant crest, own itself beaten and go
pouring by in great foaming waves on either hand,
you see nothing, you hear nothing of the toiling
engines, the reeking stokers, the effort and the
stress below; you beat west and west, as the sun
does and it might seem with nearly the same independence of any living man's help or opposition.
Equally so does it seem this great, gleaming, confident thing of power and metal came inevitably
out of the past and will lead on to still more shining,
still swifter and securer monsters in the future.

MATERIAL PROGRESS

One sees in the perspective of history, first the
little cockle-shells of Columbus, the comings and
goings of the precarious Tudor adventurers, the
slow uncertain shipping of colonial days. Says Sir
George Trevelyan in the opening of his *American
Revolution*, that then — it is still not a century
and a half ago!—

"a man bound for New York, as he sent his luggage on
board at Bristol, would willingly have compounded for
a voyage lasting as many weeks as it now lasts days. . . .
Adams, during the height of the war, hurrying to France
in the finest frigate Congress could place at his disposal
. . . could make not better speed than five and forty days
between Boston and Bordeaux. Lord Carlisle . . . was six
weeks between port and port; tossed by gales which in-
flicted on his brother Commissioners agonies such as he for-
bore to make a matter of joke even to George Selwyn. . . .
How humbler individuals fared. . . . They would be kept
waiting weeks on the wrong side of the water for a full
complement of passengers and weeks more for a fair wind,
and then beating across in a badly found tub with a cargo
of millstones and old iron rolling about below, they thought
themselves lucky if they came into harbor a month after
their private store of provisions had run out and carrying
a budget of news as stale as the ship's provisions."

Even in the time of Dickens things were by no
measure more than half - way better. I have with
me to enhance my comfort by this aided retro-
spect, his *American Notes*. His crossing lasted
eighteen days and his boat was that "far - famed
American steamer," the *Britannia* (the first of the
long succession of Cunarders, of which this *Carmania*

is the latest); his return took fifty days, and was a jovial home - coming under sail. It's the journey out gives us our contrast. He had the "state-room" of the period and very unhappy he was in it, as he testifies in a characteristically mounting passage.

"That this state - room had been specially engaged for 'Charles Dickens, Esquire, and Lady,' was rendered sufficiently clear even to my scared intellect by a very small manuscript, announcing the fact, which was pinned on a very flat quilt, covering a very thin mattress, spread like a surgical plaster on a most inaccessible shelf. But that this was the state-room, concerning which Charles Dickens, Esquire, and Lady, had held daily and nightly conferences for at least four months preceding; that this could by any possibility be that small snug chamber of the imagination, which Charles Dickens, Esquire, with the spirit of prophecy strong upon him, had always foretold would contain at least one little sofa, and which his Lady, with a modest and yet most magnificent sense of its limited dimensions, had from the first opined would not hold more than two enormous portmanteaus in some odd corner out of sight (portmanteaus which could now no more be got in at the door, not to say stowed away, than a giraffe could be persuaded or forced into a flower-pot): that this utterly impracticable, thoroughly preposterous box, had the remotest reference to, or connection with, those chaste and pretty bowers, sketched in a masterly hand, in the highly varnished, lithographic plan, hanging up in the agent's counting-house in the City of London: that this room of state, in short, could be anything but a pleasant fiction and cheerful jest of the Captain's, invented and put in practice for the better relish and enjoyment of the real state-room presently to be disclosed: these were truths which I really could not bring my mind at all to bear upon or comprehend."

MATERIAL PROGRESS

So he precludes his two weeks and a half of vile weather in this paddle boat of the middle ages (she carried a "formidable" multitude of no less than eighty-six saloon passengers) and goes on to describe such experiences as this;

"About midnight we shipped a sea, which forced its way through the skylights, burst open the doors above, and came raging and roaring down into the ladies' cabin, to the unspeakable consternation of my wife and a little Scotch lady. . . . They, and the handmaid before mentioned, being in such ecstacies of fear that I scarcely knew what to do with them, I naturally bethought myself of some restorative or comfortable cordial; and nothing better occurring to me, at the moment, than hot brandy-and-water, I procured a tumblerful without delay. It being impossible to stand or sit without holding on, they were all heaped together in one corner of a long sofa—a fixture extending entirely across the cabin—where they clung to each other in momentary expectation of being drowned. When I approached this place with my specific, and was about to administer it with many consolatory expressions, to the nearest sufferer, what was my dismay to see them all roll slowly down to the other end! and when I staggered to that end, and held out the glass once more, how immensely baffled were my good intentions by the ship giving another lurch, and their rolling back again! I suppose I dodged them up and down this sofa, for at least a quarter of an hour, without reaching them once; and by the time I did catch them, the brandy-and-water was diminished, by constant spilling, to a teaspoonful. To complete the group, it is necessary to recognize in this disconcerted dodger, an individual very pale from sea-sickness, who had shaved his beard and brushed his hair last at Liverpool; and whose only articles of dress (linen not included) were a pair of dreadnought trousers; a blue jacket, formerly admired upon the Thames at Richmond; no stockings; and one slipper."

27

It gives one a momentary sense of superiority to the great master to read that. One surveys one's immediate surroundings and compares them with *his*. One says almost patronizingly: "Poor old Dickens, you know, really did have too awful a time!" The waves are high now, and getting higher, dark-blue waves foam-crested; the waves haven't altered—except relatively—but one isn't even sea-sick. At the most there are squeamish moments for the weaker brethren. One looks down on these long white-crested undulations thirty feet or so of rise and fall, as we look down the side of a sky-scraper into a tumult in the street.

We displace thirty thousand tons of water instead of twelve hundred, we can carry 521 first and second class passengers, a crew of 463, and 2260 emigrants below. . . .

We're a city rather than a ship, our funnels go up over the height of any reasonable church spire, and you need walk the main-deck from end to end and back only four times to do a mile. Any one who has been to London and seen Trafalgar Square will get our dimensions perfectly, when he realizes that we should only squeeze into that finest site in Europe, diagonally, dwarfing the National Gallery, St. Martin's Church, hotels and every other building there out of existence, our funnels towering five feet higher than Nelson on his column. As one looks down on it all from the boat-deck one has a social microcosm, we could set up as a small modern

28

country and renew civilization even if the rest of the world was destroyed. We've the plutocracy up here, there is a middle class on the second-class deck and forward a proletariat—the *proles* much in evidence—complete. It's possible to go slumming aboard. . . . We have our daily paper, too, printed aboard, and all the latest news by marconigram. . . .

Never was anything of this sort before, never. Caligula's shipping it is true (unless it was Constantine's) did, as Mr. Cecil Torr testifies, hold a world record until the nineteenth century and he quotes Pliny for thirteen hundred tons—outdoing the *Britannia*—and Moschion for cabins and baths and covered vine-shaded walks and plants in pots. But from 1840 onward, we have broken away into a new scale for life. This *Carmania* isn't the largest ship nor the finest, nor is it to be the last. Greater ships are to follow and greater. The scale of size, the scale of power, the speed and dimensions of things about us alter remorselessly—to some limit we cannot at present descry.

III

IT is the development of such things *Is Progress Inevitable?* as this, it is this dramatically abbreviated perspective from those pre-Reformation caravels to the larger, larger, larger of the present vessels, one must blame for one's illusions.

29

One is led unawares to believe that this something called Progress is a natural and necessary and secular process, going on without the definite will of man, carrying us on quite independently of us; one is led unawa es to forget that it is after all from the historical point of view only a sudden universal jolting forward in history, an affair of two centuries at most, a process for the continuance of which we have no sort of guarantee. Most western Europeans have this delusion of automatic progress in things badly enough, but with Americans it seems to be almost fundamental. It is their theory of the Cosmos and they no more think of inquiring into the sustaining causes of the progressive movement than they would into the character of the stokers hidden away from us in this great thing somewhere — the officers alone know where.

I am happy to find this blind confidence very well expressed for example in an illustrated magazine article by Mr. Edgar Saltus, "New York from the Flat-iron," that a friend has put in my hand to prepare me for the wonders to come. Mr. Saltus writes with an eloquent joy of his vision of Broadway below, Broadway that is now "barring trade-routes, the largest commercial stretch on this planet." So late as Dickens's visit it was scavenged by roving untended herds of gaunt, brown, black-blotched pigs. He writes of lower Fifth Avenue and upper Fifth Avenue, of Madison Square and its tower, of sky-scrapers and sky-scrapers and sky-scrapers round and about the horizon. (I am to have a tremendous view of them to-morrow as we steam up from the Narrows.) And thus Mr. Saltus proceeds,—

"As you lean and gaze from the toppest floors on houses below, which from those floors seem huts, it may occur to you that precisely as these huts were once regarded as supreme achievements, so, one of these days, from other and higher floors, the Flat-iron may seem a hut itself. Evolution has not halted. Undiscernibly but indefatigably, always it is progressing. Its final term is not existing buildings, nor in existing man. If humanity sprang from gorillas, from humanity gods shall proceed."

The rule of three in excelsis!

"The story of Olympus is merely a tale of what might have been. That which might have been may yet come to pass. Even now could the old divinities, hushed forevermore, awake, they would be perplexed enough to see how mortals have exceeded them. . . . In Fifth Avenue inns they could get fairer fare than ambrosia, and behold women beside whom Venus herself would look provincial and Juno a frump. The spectacle of electricity tamed and domesticated would surprise them not a little, the elevated quite as much, the Flat-iron still more. At sight of the latter they would recall the Titans with whom once they warred, and sink to their sun-red seas outfaced.

"In this same measure we have succeeded in exceeding them, so will posterity surpass what we have done. Evolution may be slow, it achieved an unrecognized advance when it devised buildings such as this. It is demonstrable that small rooms breed small thoughts. It will be demonstrable that, as buildings ascend, so do ideas. It is mental progress that sky-scrapers engender. From these parturitions gods may really proceed—beings, that is, who, could we remain long enough to see them, would regard us as we regard the apes. . . ."

Mr. Saltus writes, I think, with a very typical American accent. Most Americans think like that and all of them I fancy feel like it. Just in that spirit a later-empire Roman might have written apropos the gigantic new basilica of Constantine the Great (who was also, one recalls, a record-breaker in ship-building) and have compared it with the straitened proportions of Cæsar's Forum and the meagre relics of republican Rome. So too (*absit omen*) he might have swelled into prophecy and sounded the true modern note.

One hears that modern note everywhere nowadays where print spreads, but from America with fewer undertones than anywhere. Even I find it, ringing clear, as a thing beyond disputing, as a thing as self-evident as sunrise again and again in the expressed thought of Mr. Henry James.

But you know this progress isn't guaranteed. We have all indeed been carried away completely by the up-rush of it all. To me now this *Carmania* seems to typify the whole thing. What matter it if there are moments when one reflects on the mysterious smallness and it would seem the ungrowing quality of the human content of it all? We are, after all, astonishingly like flies on a machine that has got loose. No matter. Those people on the main-deck are the oddest crowd, strange Oriental-looking figures with Astrakhan caps, hook - noses, shifty eyes, and indisputably dirty habits, bold-eyed, red-capped, expectorating women, quaint and amazingly dirty children; Tartars there are too, and Cossacks, queer wraps, queer head-dresses, a sort of greasy picturesqueness over them all. They use the handkerchief solely as a head covering. Their deck is disgusting with fragments of food, with egg-shells they haven't had the decency to throw over-board. Collectively they have — an atmosphere. They're going where we're going, wherever that is. What matters it? What matters it, too, if these people about me in the artistic apartment talk noth-ing but trivialities derived from the *Daily Bulletin*, think nothing but trivialities, are, except in the capacity of paying passengers, the most ineffectual gathering of human beings conceivable? What matters it that there is no connection, no under-standing whatever between them and that large and ominous crowd a plank or so and a yard or so under our feet? Or between themselves for the matter of that? What matters it if nobody seems to be struck by the fact that we are all, the three thousand two hundred of us so extraordinarily got together into this tremendous machine, and that not only does nobody inquire what it is has got us together in this astonishing fashion and why, but that no-body seems to feel that we are together in any sort of way at all? One looks up at the smoke-pouring funnels and back at the foaming wake. It will be all right. Aren't we driving ahead westward at a pace of four hundred and fifty miles a day?

And twenty or thirty thousand other souls, mixed and stratified, on great steamers ahead of us, or behind, are driving westward too. That there's no collective mind apparent in it at all, worth speaking about is so much the better. That only shows its Destiny, its Progress as inevitable as gravitation. I could almost believe it, as I sit quietly writing here by a softly shaded light in this elegantly appointed drawing-room, as steady as though I was in my native habitat on dry land instead of hurrying almost fearfully, at twenty knots an hour, over a tumbling empty desert of blue waves under a windy sky. But, only a little while ago, I was out forward alone, looking at that. Everything was still except for the remote throbbing of the engines and the nearly effaced sound of a man, singing in a strange tongue, that came from the third-class gangway far below. The sky was clear, save for a few black streamers of clouds, Orion hung very light and large above the waters, and a great new moon, still visibly holding its dead predecessor in its crescent, sank near him. Between the sparse great stars were deep blue spaces, unfathomed distances.

Out there I had been reminded of space and time. Out there the ship was just a hastening ephemeral fire-fly that had chanced to happen across the eternal tumult of the winds and sea.

CHAPTER III

NEW YORK

(In a room on the ninth floor in the sky-scraper hotel New York)

I

First Impressions My first impressions of New York are enormously to enhance the effect of this Progress, this material progress, that is to say, as something inevitable and inhuman, as a blindly furious energy of growth that must go on. Against the broad and level gray contours of Liverpool one found the ocean liner portentously tall, but here one steams into the middle of a town that dwarfs the ocean liner. The sky-scrapers that are the New-Yorker's perpetual boast and pride rise up to greet one as one comes through the Narrows into the Upper Bay, stand out, in a clustering group of tall irregular crenellations, the strangest crown that ever a city wore. They have an effect of immense incompleteness; each one seems to await some needed terminal,—to be, by virtue of its woolly jets of steam, still as it were in process of eruption. One thinks of St. Peter's great blue dome, finished and done as one saw it from a vine-shaded wine-booth above the Milvian Bridge, one thinks of the sudden ascendency of St. Paul's dark grace, as it soars out over any one who comes up by the Thames towards it. These are efforts that have accomplished their ends, and even Paris illuminated under the tall stem of the Eiffel Tower looked completed and defined. But New York's achievement is a threatening promise, growth going on under a pressure that increases, and amidst a hungry uproar of effort.

One gets a measure of the quality of this force of mechanical, of inhuman, growth as one marks the great statue of Liberty on our larboard, which is meant to dominate and fails absolutely to dominate the scene. It gets to three hundred feet about, by standing on a pedestal of a hundred and fifty; and the uplifted torch, seen against the sky, suggests an arm straining upward, straining in hopeless competition with the fierce commercial altitudes ahead. Poor liberating Lady of the American ideal! One passes her and forgets.

Happy returning natives greet the great pillars of business by name, the St. Paul Building, the World, the Manhattan tower; the English new-comer notes the clear emphasis of the detail, the freedom from smoke and atmospheric mystery that New York gains from burning anthracite, the jetting white steam clouds that emphasize that freedom. Across the broad harbor plies an unfamiliar traffic of grotesque broad ferry-boats, black with people, glutted to the lips with vans and carts, each hooting and yelping its own distinctive note, and there is a wild hurrying up and down and to and fro of piping and bellowing tugs and barges; and a great floating platform, bearing a railway train, gets athwart our course as we ascend and evokes megatherial bellowings. Everything is moving at a great speed, and whistling and howling, it seems, and presently far ahead we make out our own pier, black with expectant people, and set up our own distinctive whoop, and with the help of half a dozen furiously noisy tugs are finally lugged and butted into dock. The tugs converse by yells and whistles, it is an affair of short-tempered mechanical monsters, amidst which one watches for one's opportunity to get ashore.

Noise and human hurry and a vastness of means and collective result, rather than any vastness of achievement, is the pervading quality of New York. The great thing is the mechanical thing, the unintentional thing which is speeding up all these people, driving them in headlong hurry this way and that, exhorting them by the voice of every car conductor to "step lively," aggregating them into shoving and elbowing masses, making them stand clinging to straps, jerking them up elevator shafts and pouring them on to the ferry-boats. But this accidental great thing is at times a very great thing. Much more impressive than the sky-scrapers to my mind is the large Brooklyn suspension-bridge. I have never troubled to ask who built that; its greatness is not in its design, but in the quality of necessity one perceives in its inanimate immensity. It *tells*, as one goes under it up the East River, but it is far more impressive to the stranger to come upon it by glimpses, wandering down to it through the ill-paved van-infested streets from Chatham Square. One sees parts of Cyclopean stone arches, one gets suggestive glimpses through the jungle growth of business now of the back, now of the flanks, of the monster; then, as one comes out on the river, one discovers far up in one's sky the long sweep of the bridge itself, foreshortened and with a maximum of perspective effect; the streams of pedestrians and the long line of carts and vans, quaintly microscopic against the blue, the creeping progress of the little cars on the lower edge of the long chain of netting; all these things dwindling indistinguishably before Brooklyn is reached. Thence, if it is late afternoon, one may walk back to City Hall Park and encounter and experience the convergent stream of clerks and workers making for the bridge, mark it grow denser and denser, until at last they come near choking even the broad approaches of the giant duct, until the congested multitudes jostle and fight for a way. They arrive marching afoot by every street in endless procession; crammed trolley-cars disgorge them; the Subway pours them out. . . . The individuals count for nothing, they are clerks and stenographers, shopmen, shop-girls, workers of innumerable types, black-

ENTRANCE TO BROOKLYN BRIDGE

coated men, hat-and-blouse girls, shabby and cheap-
ly clad persons, such as one sees in London, in Berlin, anywhere. Perhaps they hurry more, perhaps
they seem more eager. But the distinctive effect
is the mass, the black torrent, rippled with unmeaning faces, the great, the unprecedented mul-
titudinousness of the thing, the inhuman force of
it all.

I made no efforts to present any of my letters, or
to find any one to talk to on my first day in New
York. I landed, got a casual lunch, and wandered
alone until New York's peculiar effect of inhuman
noise and pressure and growth became overwhelming, touched me with a sense of solitude, and drove
me into the hospitable companionship of the Century Club. Oh, no doubt of New York's immensity!
The sense of soulless gigantic forces, that took no
heed of men, became stronger and stronger all that
day. The pavements were often almost incredibly
out of repair, when I became footweary the street-
cars would not wait for me, and I had to learn their
stopping - points as best I might. I wandered,
just at the right pitch of fatigue to get the full
force of it into the eastward region between Third
and Fourth Avenue, came upon the Elevated railway at its worst, the darkened streets of disordered
paving below, trolley-car-congested, the ugly clumsy
lattice, sonorously busy overhead, a clatter of vans
and draught-horses, and great crowds of cheap, base-
looking people hurrying uncivilly by. . . .

II

I CORRECTED that first crowded impression of New York with a clearer, brighter vision of expansiveness when next day I began to realize the social quality of New York's central backbone, between Fourth Avenue and Sixth. The effect remained still that of an immeasurably powerful forward movement of rapid eager advance, a process of enlargement and increment in every material sense, but it may be because I was no longer fatigued, was now a little initiated, the human being seemed less of a fly upon the wheels. I visited immense and magnificent clubs—London has no such splendors as the Union, the University, the new hall of the Harvard—I witnessed the great torrent of spending and glittering prosperity in carriage and motor-car pour along Fifth Avenue. I became aware of effects that were not only vast and opulent but fine. It grew upon me that the Twentieth Century, which found New York brown-stone of the color of desiccated chocolate, meant to leave it a city of white and colored marble. I found myself agape, admiring a sky-scraper—the prow of the Flat-iron Building, to be particular, ploughing up through the traffic of Broadway and Fifth Avenue in the afternoon light. The New York sundown and twilight seemed to me quite glorious things. Down the western streets one gets the sky hung in long cloud-barred strips, like Japanese paintings, celestial tranquil yellows and greens and pink luminosity toning down to the reeking blue-brown edge of the distant New Jersey atmosphere, and the clear, black, hard activity of crowd and trolley-car and Elevated railroad. Against this deepening color came the innumerable little lights of the house cliffs and the street tier above tier. New York is lavish of light, it is lavish of everything, it is full of the sense of spending from an inexhaustible supply. For a time one is drawn irresistibly into the universal belief in that inexhaustible supply.

At a bright table in Delmonico's to-day at lunch-time, my host told me the first news of the destruction of the great part of San Francisco by earthquake and fire. It had just come through to him, it wasn't yet being shouted by the newsboys. He told me compactly of dislocated water-mains, of the ill-luck of the unusual eastward wind that was blowing the fire up-town, of a thousand reported dead, of the manifest doom of the greater portion of the city, and presently the shouting voices in the street outside arose to chorus him. He was a newspaper man and a little preoccupied because his San Francisco offices were burning, and that no further news was arriving after these first intimations. Naturally the catastrophe was our topic. But this disaster did not affect him, it does not seem to have affected any one with a sense of final destruction, with any foreboding of irreparable disaster. Every one is

41

talking of it this afternoon, and no one is in the least degree dismayed. I have talked and listened in two clubs, watched people in cars and in the street, and one man is glad that Chinatown will be cleared out for good; another's chief solicitude is for Millet's "Man with the Hoe." "They'll cut it out of the frame," he says, a little anxiously. "Sure." But there is no doubt anywhere that San Francisco can be rebuilt, larger, better, and soon. Just as there would be none at all if all this New York that has so obsessed me with its limitless bigness was itself a blazing ruin. I believe these people would more than half like the situation. It would give them scope, it would facilitate that conversion into white marble in progress everywhere, it would settle the difficulties of the Elevated railroad and clear out the tangles of lower New York. There is no sense of accomplishment and finality in any of these things, the largest, the finest, the tallest, are so obviously no more than symptoms and promises of Material Progress, of inhuman material progress that is so in the nature of things that no one would regret their passing. That, I say again, is at the first encounter the peculiar American effect that began directly I stepped aboard the liner, and that rises here to a towering, shining, clamorous climax. The sense of inexhaustible supply, of an ultra - human force behind it all, is, for a time, invincible.

One assumes, with Mr. Saltus, that all America is in this vein, and that this is the way the future must inevitably go. One has a vision of bright electrical subways, replacing the filth-diffusing railways of to-day, of clean, clear pavements free altogether from the fly-prolific filth of horses coming almost, as it were, of their own accord beneath the feet of a population that no longer expectorates at all; of grimy stone and peeling paint giving way everywhere to white marble and spotless surfaces, and a shining order, of everything wider, taller, cleaner, better. . . .

So that, in the meanwhile, a certain amount of jostling and hurry and untidiness, and even—to put it mildly—forcefulness may be forgiven.

III

I VISITED Ellis Island yesterday. It
Ellis Island chanced to be a good day for my purpose. For the first time in its history this filter of immigrant humanity has this week proved inadequate to the demand upon it. It was choked, and half a score of gravid liners were lying uncomfortably up the harbor, replete with twenty thousand or so of crude Americans from Ireland and Poland and Italy and Syria and Finland and Albania; men, women, children, dirt, and bags together.

Of immigration I shall have to write later; what concerns me now is chiefly the wholesale and multitudinous quality of that place and its work. I made my way with my introduction along white

43

passages and through traps and a maze of metal lattices that did for a while succeed in catching and imprisoning me, to Commissioner Wachorn, in his quiet, green-toned office. There, for a time, I sat judicially and heard him deal methodically, swiftly, sympathetically, with case after case, a string of appeals against the sentences of deportation pronounced in the busy little courts below. First would come one dingy and strangely garbed group of wild-eyed aliens, and then another: Roumanian gypsies, South Italians, Ruthenians, Swedes, each under the intelligent guidance of a uniformed interpreter, and a case would be started, a report made to Washington, and they would drop out again, hopeful or sullen or fearful as the evidence might trend. . . .

Down-stairs we find the courts, and these seen, we traverse long refectories, long aisles of tables, and close - packed dormitories with banks of steel mattresses, tier above tier, and galleries and passages innumerable, perplexing intricacy that slowly grows systematic with the Commissioner's explanations.

Here is a huge, gray, untidy waiting-room, like a big railway-depot room, full of a sinister crowd of miserable people, loafing about or sitting dejectedly, whom America refuses, and here a second and a third such chamber each with its tragic and evil-looking crowd that hates us, and that even ventures to groan and hiss at us a little for our glimpse of its large dirty spectacle of hopeless failure, and here, squalid enough indeed, but still to some degree hopeful, are the appeal cases as yet undecided. In one place, at a bank of ranges, works an army of men cooks, in another spins the big machinery of the Ellis Island laundry, washing blankets, drying blankets, day in and day out, a big clean steamy space of hurry and rotation. Then, I recall a neat apartment lined to the ceiling with little drawers, a card-index of the names and nationalities and significant circumstances of upward of a million and a half of people who have gone on and who are yet liable to recall.

The central hall is the key of this impression. All day long, through an intricate series of metal pens, the long procession files, step by step, bearing bundles and trunks and boxes, past this examiner and that, past the quick, alert medical officers, the tallymen and the clerks. At every point immigrants are being picked out and set aside for further medical examination, for further questions, for the busy little courts; but the main procession satisfies conditions, passes on. It is a daily procession that, with a yard of space to each, would stretch over three miles, that any week in the year would more than equal in numbers that daily procession of the unemployed that is becoming a regular feature of the London winter, that in a year could put a cordon round London or New York of close-marching people, could populate a new Boston, that in a century— What in a century will it all amount to? . . .

On they go, from this pen to that, pen by pen,

towards a desk at a little metal wicket—the gate of America. Through this metal wicket drips the immigration stream—all day long, every two or three seconds an immigrant, with a valise or a bundle, passes the little desk and goes on past the well-managed money-changing place, past the carefully organized separating ways that go to this railway or that, past the guiding, protecting officials—into a new world. The great majority are young men and young women, between seventeen and thirty, good, youthful, hopeful, peasant stock. They stand in a long string, waiting to go through that wicket, with bundles, with little tin boxes, with cheap portmanteaus, with odd packages, in pairs, in families, alone, women with children, men with strings of dependents, young couples. All day that string of human beads waits there, jerks forward, waits again; all day and every day, constantly replenished, constantly dropping the end beads through the wicket, till the units mount to hundreds and the hundreds to thousands. . . .

Yes, Ellis Island is quietly immense. It gives one a visible image of one aspect at least of this world-large process of filling and growing and synthesis, which is America.

"Look there!" said the Commissioner, taking me by the arm and pointing, and I saw a monster steamship far away, and already a big bulk looming up the Narrows. "It's the *Kaiser Wilhelm der Grosse*. She's got—I forget the exact figures, but let us say—eight hundred and fifty-three more for us. She'll have to keep them until Friday at the earliest. And there's more behind her, and more strung out all across the Atlantic."

In one record day this month 21,000 immigrants came into the port of New York alone; in one week over 50,000. This year the total will be 1,200,000 souls, pouring in, finding work at once, producing no fall in wages. They start digging and building and making. Just think of the dimensions of it!

IV

ONE must get away from New York
To Fall River to see the place in its proper relations.

I visited Staten Island and Jersey City, motored up to Sleepy Hollow (where once the Headless Horseman rode), saw suburbs and intimations of suburbs without end, and finished with the long and crowded spectacle of the East River as one sees it from the Fall River boat. It was Friday night, and the Fall River boat was in a state of fine congestion with Jews, Italians, and week-enders, and one stood crowded and surveyed the crowded shore, the sky - scrapers and tenement - houses, the huge grain elevators, big warehouses, the great Brooklyn Bridge, the still greater Williamsburgh Bridge, the great promise of yet another monstrous bridge, overwhelmingly monstrous by any European example I know, and so past long miles of city to the left and to the right past the wide Brooklyn navy-yard (where three clean white war-ships lay moored), past the clustering castellated asylums, hospitals, almshouses and reformatories of Blackwell's long shore and Ward's Island, and then through a long reluctant diminuendo on each receding bank, until, indeed, New York, though it seemed incredible, had done.

And at one point a grave-voiced man in a peaked cap, with guide-books to sell, pleased me greatly by ending all idle talk suddenly with the stentorian announcement: "We are now in Hell Gate. We are now passing through Hell Gate!"

But they've blown Hell Gate open with dynamite, and it wasn't at all the Hell Gate that I read about in my boyhood in the delightful chronicle of Knickerbocker.

So through an elbowing evening (to the tune of "Cavalleria Rusticana" on an irrepressible string band) and a night of unmitigated fog-horn to Boston, which I had been given to understand was a cultured and uneventful city offering great opportunities for reflection and intellectual digestion. And, indeed, the large quiet of Beacon Street, in the early morning sunshine, seemed to more than justify that expectation. . . .

CHAPTER IV

GROWTH INVINCIBLE

I

Boston's Way of Growing BUT Boston did not propose that its less-assertive key should be misunderstood, and in a singularly short space of time I found myself climbing into a tremulous impatient motor-car in company with three enthusiastic exponents of the work of the Metropolitan Park Commission, and provided with a neatly tinted map, large and framed and glazed, to explore a fresh and more deliberate phase in this great American symphony, this symphony of Growth.

If possible it is more impressive, even, than the crowded largeness of New York, to trace the serene preparation Boston has made through this Commission to be widely and easily vast. New York's humanity has a curious air of being carried along upon a wave of irresistible prosperity, but Boston confesses design. I suppose no city in all the world (unless it be Washington) has ever produced so complete and ample a forecast of its own future as this Commission's plan of Boston. An area with a radius of between fifteen and twenty miles from the State House has been planned out and prepared for Growth. Great reservations of woodland and hill have been made, the banks of nearly all the streams and rivers and meres have been secured for public park and garden, for boating and other water sports big avenues of vigorous young trees; a hundred and fifty yards or so wide, with drive-ways and ridingways and a central grassy band for electric tramways, have been prepared, and, indeed, the fair and ample and shady new Boston, the Boston of 1950, grows visibly before one's eyes. I found myself comparing the disciplined confidence of these proposals to the blind enlargement of London; London, that like a bowl of viscid human fluid, boils sullenly over the rim of its encircling hills and slops messily and uglily into the home counties. I could not but contrast their large intelligence with the confused hesitations and waste and muddle of our English suburban developments. . . .

There were moments, indeed, when it seemed too good to be true, and Mr. Sylvester Baxter, who was with me and whose faith has done so much to se-cure this mapping out of a city's growth beyond all precedent, became the victim of my doubts. "Will this enormous space of sunlit woodland and marsh and meadow really be filled at any time?" I urged. "All cities do not grow. Cities have shrunken."

I recalled Bruges. I recalled the empty, goat-sustaining, flower-rich meadows of Rome within the wall. What made him so sure of this progressive magnificence of Boston's growth? My doubts fell on stony soil. My companions seemed to think these scepticisms inopportune, a forced eccentricity, like doubting the coming of to-morrow. Of course Growth will go on. . . .

The subject was changed by the sight of the fine marble buildings of the Harvard medical school, a shining façade partially eclipsed by several dingy and unsightly wooden houses.

"These shanties will go, of course," says one of my companions. "It's proposed to take the avenue right across this space straight to the schools."

"You'll have to fill the marsh, then, and buy the houses."

"Sure." . . .

I find myself comparing this huge growth process of America with the things in my own land. After all, this growth is no distinctive American thing; it is the same process anywhere—only in America there are no disguises, no complications. Come to think of it, Birmingham and Manchester are as new as Boston—newer; and London, south and east of the Thames, is, save for a little nucleus, more recent than Chicago—is in places, I am told, with its smoky disorder, its clattering ways, its brutality of industrial conflict, very like Chicago. But nowhere now is growth still so certainly and confidently *going on* as here. Nowhere is it upon so great a

scale as here, and with so confident an outlook towards the things to come. And nowhere is it passing more certainly from the first phase of a mob-
like rush of individualistic undertakings into a
planned and ordered progress.

II

EVERYWHERE in the America I have
The End of
Niagara   seen the same note sounds, the note
of a fatal gigantic economic development, of large prevision and enormous pressures.

I heard it clear above the roar of Niagara—for,
after all, I stopped off at Niagara.

As a water-fall, Niagara's claim to distinction is
now mainly quantitative; its spectacular effect, its
magnificent and humbling size and splendor, were
long since destroyed beyond recovery by the hotels,
the factories, the power-houses, the bridges and
tramways and hoardings that arose about it. It
must have been a fine thing to happen upon suddenly after a day of solitary travel; the Indians,
they say, gave it worship; but it's no great wonder
to reach it by trolley-car, through a street hack-
infested and full of adventurous refreshment-places
and souvenir-shops and the touting guides. There
were great quantities of young couples and other
sight-seers with the usual encumbrances of wrap
and bag and umbrella, trailing out across the

bridges and along the neat paths of the Reservation Parks, asking the way to this point and that. Notice boards cut the eye, offering extra joys and memorable objects for twenty-five and fifty cents, and it was proposed you should keep off the grass.

After all, the gorge of Niagara is very like any good gorge in the Ardennes, except that it has more water; it's about as wide and about as deep, and there is no effect at all that one has not seen a dozen times in other cascades. One gets all the water one wants at Tivoli, one has gone behind half a hundred downpours just as impressive in Switzerland; a hundred tons of water is really just as stunning as ten million. A hundred tons of water stuns one altogether, and what more do you want? One recalls "Orridos" and "Schluchts" that are not only magnificent but lonely.

No doubt the Falls, seen from the Canadian side, have a peculiar long majesty of effect; but the finest thing in it all, to my mind, was not Niagara at all, but to look up-stream from Goat Island and see the sea-wide crest of the flashing sunlit rapids against the gray-blue sky. That was like a limitless ocean pouring down a sloping world towards one, and I lingered, held by that, returning to it through an indolent afternoon. It gripped the imagination as nothing else there seemed to do. It was so broad an infinitude of splash and hurry. And, moreover, all the enterprising hotels and expectant trippers were out of sight.

That was the best of the display. The real interest of Niagara for me, was not in the water-fall but in the human accumulations about it. They stood for the future, threats and promises, and the water-fall was just a vast reiteration of falling water. The note of growth in human accomplishment rose clear and triumphant above the elemental thunder.

For the most part these accumulations of human effort about Niagara are extremely defiling and ugly. Nothing—not even the hotel signs and advertisement boards—could be more offensive to the eye and mind than the Schoellkopf Company's untidy confusion of sheds and buildings on the American side, wastefully squirting out long, tail-race cascades below the bridge, and nothing more disgusting than the sewer-pipes and gas-work ooze that the town of Niagara Falls contributes to the scenery. But, after all, these represent only the first slovenly onslaught of mankind's expansion, the pioneers' camp of the human-growth process that already changes its quality and manner. There are finer things than these outrages to be found.

The dynamos and turbines of the Niagara Falls Power Company, for example, impressed me far more profoundly than the Cave of the Winds; are, indeed, to my mind, greater and more beautiful than that accidental eddying of air beside a downpour. They are will made visible, thought translated into easy and commanding things. They are clean, noiseless, and starkly powerful. All the clatter and tumult of the early age of machinery is past and gone here; there is no smoke, no coal grit, no dirt at all. The wheel-pit into which one descends has an almost cloistered quiet about its softly humming turbines. These are altogether noble masses of machinery, huge black slumbering monsters, great sleeping tops that engender irresistible forces in their sleep. They sprang, armed like Minerva, from serene and speculative, foreseeing and endeavoring brains. First was the word and then these powers. A man goes to and fro quietly in the long, clean hall of the dynamos. There is no clangor, no racket. Yet the outer rim of the big generators is spinning at the pace of a hundred thousand miles an hour; the dazzling clean switchboard, with its little handles and levers, is the seat of empire over more power than the strength of a million disciplined, unquestioning men. All these great things are as silent, as wonderfully made, as the heart in a living body, and stouter and stronger than that. . . .

When I thought that these two huge wheel-pits of this company are themselves but a little intimation of what can be done in this way, what will be done in this way, my imagination towered above me. I fell into a day-dream of the coming power of men, and how that power may be used by them. . . .

For surely the greatness of life is still to come, it is not in such accidents as mountains or the sea. I have seen the splendor of the mountains, sunrise and sunset among them, and the waste immensity of sky and sea. I am not blind because I can see beyond these glories. To me no other thing is credible than that all the natural beauty in the world is only so much material for the imagination and the mind, so many hints and suggestions for art and creation. Whatever is, is but the lure and symbol towards what can be willed and done. Man lives to make—in the end he must make, for there will be nothing else left for him to do.

And the world he will make—after a thousand years or so!

I, at least, can forgive the loss of all the accidental, unmeaning beauty that is going for the sake of the beauty of fine order and intention that will come. I believe—passionately, as a doubting lover believes in his mistress — in the future of mankind. And so to me it seems altogether well that all the froth and hurry of Niagara at last, all of it, dying into hungry canals of intake, should rise again in light and power, in ordered and equipped and proud and beautiful humanity, in cities and palaces and the emancipated souls and hearts of men. . . .

I turned back to look at the power-house as I walked towards the Falls, and halted and stared. Its architecture brought me out of my day-dream to the quality of contemporary things again. It's a well-intentioned building enough, extraordinarily well intentioned, and regardless of expense. It's in granite and by Stanford White, and yet— It hasn't caught the note. There's a touch of respectability in it, more than a hint of the box of bricks. Odd, but I'd almost as soon have had one of the Schoellkopf sheds.

A community that can produce such things as those turbines and dynamos, and then cover them over with this dull exterior, is capable, one realizes, of feats of bathos. One feels that all the power that throbs in the copper cables below may end at last in turning Great Wheels for excursionists, stamping out aluminum "fancy" ware, and illuminating night advertisements for drug shops and music halls. I had an afternoon of busy doubts. . . .

There is much discussion about Niagara at present. It may be some queer compromise, based on the pretence that a voluminous water-fall is necessarily a thing of incredible beauty, and a human use is necessarily a degrading use, will "save" Niagara and the hack-drivers and the souvenir-shops for series of years yet, "a magnificent monument to the pride of the United States in a glory of nature," as one journalistic savior puts it. It is, as public opinion stands, a quite conceivable thing. This electric development may be stopped after all, and the huge fall of water remain surrounded by gravel paths and parapets and geranium-beds, a staring-point for dull wonder, a crown for a day's excursion, a thunderous impressive accessory to the vulgar love - making that fills the surrounding hotels, a Titanic imbecility of wasted gifts. But I don't think so. I think somebody will pay something, and the journalistic zeal for scenery abate. I think the huge social and industrial process of America will win in this conflict, and at last capture Niagara altogether.

And then—what use will it make of its prey?

III

In smoky, vast, undisciplined Chicago
The Tail of
Chicago Growth forced itself upon me again as the dominant American fact, but this time a dark disorder of growth. I went about Chicago seeing many things of which I may say something later. I visited the top of the Masonic Building and viewed a wilderness of sky-scrapers. I acquired a felt of memories of swing bridges and viaducts and interlacing railways and jostling crowds and extraordinarily dirty streets, I learnt something of the mystery of the "floating foundations" upon which so much of Chicago rests. But I got my best vision of Chicago as I left it.

I sat in the open observation-car at the end of the Pennsylvania Limited Express, and watched the long defile of industrialism from the Union Station in the heart of things to out beyond South

Chicago, a dozen miles away. I had not gone to the bloody spectacle of the stock-yards that "feed the world," because, to be frank, I have an immense repugnance to the killing of fixed and helpless animals; I saw nothing of those ill-managed, ill-inspected establishments, though I smelt the unwholesome reek from them ever and again, and so it was here I saw for the first time the enormous expanse and intricacy of railroads that net this great industrial desolation, and something of the going and coming of the myriads of polyglot workers. Chicago burns bituminous coal, it has a reek that outdoes London, and right and left of the line rise vast chimneys, huge blackened grain-elevators, flame-crowned furnaces and gauntly ugly and filthy factory buildings, monstrous mounds of refuse, desolate, empty lots littered with rusty cans, old iron, and indescribable rubbish. Interspersed with these are groups of dirty, disreputable, insanitary - looking wooden houses.

We swept along the many-railed track, and the straws and scraps of paper danced in our eddy as we passed. We overtook local trains and they receded slowly in the great perspective, huge freight-trains met us or were overtaken; long trains of doomed cattle passed northward; solitary engines went by—every engine tolling a melancholy bell; open trucks crowded with workmen went cityward. By the side of the track, and over the level crossings, walked great numbers of people. So it goes on mile after mile—Chicago. The sun was now bright, now pallid through some streaming curtain of smoke; the spring afternoon was lit here and again by the gallant struggle of some stunted tree with a rare and startling note of new green. . . .

It was like a prolonged, enlarged mingling of the south side of London with all that is bleak and ugly in the Black Country. It is the most perfect presentation of nineteenth - century individualistic industrialism I have ever seen—in its vast, its magnificent squalor; it is pure nineteenth century; it had no past at all before that; in 1800 it was empty prairie, and one marvels for its future. It is indeed a nineteenth-century nightmare that culminates beyond South Chicago in the monstrous fungoid shapes, the endless smoking chimneys, the squat retorts, the black smoke pall of the Standard Oil Company. For a time the sun is veiled altogether by that. . . .

And then suddenly Chicago is a dark smear under the sky, and we are in the large emptiness of America, the other America—America in between.

IV

"Undisciplined"—that is the word
Intimations of Order for Chicago. It is the word for all the progress of the Victorian time, a scrambling, ill-mannered, undignified, unintelligent de-

velopment of material resources. Packing-town, for example, is a place that feeds the world with meat, that concentrates the produce of a splendid countryside at a position of imperial advantage, and its owners have no more sense, no better moral quality, than to make it stink in the nostrils of any one who comes within two miles of it; to make it a centre of distribution for disease and decay, an arena of shabby evasions and extra profits; a scene of brutal economic conflict and squalid filthiness, offensive to every sense. (I wish I could catch the soul of Herbert Spencer and tether it in Chicago for awhile to gather fresh evidence upon the superiority of unfettered individualistic enterprises to things managed by the state.)

Want of discipline! Chicago is one hoarse cry for discipline! The reek and scandal of the stock-yards is really only a gigantic form of that same quality in American life that, in a minor aspect, makes the sidewalk filthy. The key to the peculiar nasty ugliness of those Schoellkopf works that defile the Niagara gorge is the same quality. The detestableness of the Elevated railroads of Chicago and Boston and New York have this in common. All that is ugly in America, in Lancashire, in South and East London, in the Pas de Calais, is due to this, to the shoving unintelligent proceedings of underbred and morally obtuse men. Each man is for himself, each enterprise; there is no order, no prevision, no common and universal plan. Modern economic organization is still as yet only thinking of emerging from its first chaotic stage, the stage of lawless enterprise and insanitary aggregation, the stage of the prospector's camp. . . .

But it does emerge.

Men are makers—American men, I think, more than most men—and amidst even the catastrophic jumble of Chicago one finds the same creative forces at work that are struggling to replan a greater Boston, and that turned a waste of dumps and swamps and cabbage-gardens into Central Park, New York. Chicago also has its Parks Commission and its green avenues, its bright flower - gardens, its lakes and playing-fields. Its Midway Plaisance is in amazing contrast with the dirt, the congestion, the moral disorder of its State Street; its Field Houses do visible battle with slum and the frantic meanness of commercial folly.

Field Houses are peculiar to Chicago, and Chicago has every reason to be proud of them. I visited one that is positively within smell of the stock-yards and wedged into a district of gaunt and dirty slums. It stands in the midst of a little park, and close by it are three playing-grounds with swings and parallel bars and all manner of athletic appliances, one for little children, one for girls and women, and one for boys and youths. In the children's place is a paddling-pond of clear, clean, running water and a shaded area of frequently changed sand, and in the park was a broad asphalted arena that can be flooded

STATE STREET, CHICAGO

for skating in winter. All this is free to all comers, and free too is the Field House itself. This is a large, cool Italianate place with two or three reading-rooms—one specially arranged for children—a big discussion-hall, a big and well-equipped gymnasium, and big, free baths for men and for women. There is also a clean, bright refreshment-place where wholesome food is sold just above cost price. It was early on Friday afternoon when I saw it all, but the place was busy with children, reading, bathing, playing in a hundred different ways.

And this Field House is not an isolated philanthropic enterprise. It is just one of a number that are dotted about Chicago, mitigating and civilizing its squalor. It was not distilled by begging and charity from the stench of the stock-yards or the reek of Standard Oil. It is part of the normal work of a special taxing body created by the legislature of the State of Illinois. It is just one of the fruits upon one of the growths that spring from such persistent creative efforts as that of the Chicago City Club. It is socialism — even as its enemies declare. . . .

Even amidst the sombre uncleanliness of Chicago one sees the light of a new epoch, the coming of new conceptions, of foresight, of large collective plans and discipline to achieve them, the fresh green leaves, among all the festering manure, of the giant growths of a more orderly and more beautiful age.

V

THESE growing towns, these giant
The
Pennsylvania
Limited towns that grow up and out, that
grow orderly and splendid out of their
first chaotic beginnings, are only little patches upon
a vast expanse, upon what is still of all habitable countries the emptiest country in the world.
My long express journey from Chicago to Washington lasted a day and a night and more, I could get
sooner from my home in Kent to Italy, and yet that
was still well under a third of the way across the
continent. I spent most of my daylight time in
the fine and graceful open loggia at the end of the
observation-car or in looking out of the windows,
looking at hills and valleys, townships and quiet
places, sudden busy industrial outbreaks about coal-
mine or metal, big undisciplined rivers that spread
into swamp and lake, new forest growths, very
bright and green now, foaming up above blackened
stumps. There were many cypress-trees and trees
with white blossom and the Judas-tree, very abundant among the spring-time green. I got still more
clearly the enormous scale of this American destiny
I seek to discuss, through all that long and interesting day of transit. I measured, as it seemed to me
for the first time, the real scale of the growth process that has put a four-track road nine hundred
miles across this exuberant land and scarred every
available hill with furnace and mine.

Bigness—that's the word! The very fields and farm-buildings seem to me to have four times the size of our English farms.

Some casual suggestion of the wayside, I forget now what, set me thinking of the former days, so recent that they are yet within the lifetime of living men, when this was frontier land, when even the middle west remained to be won. I thought of the slow diffusing population of the forties, the pioneer wagon, the men armed with axe and rifle, knife and revolver, the fear of the Indians, the weak and casual incidence of law. Then the high-road was but a prairie track and all these hills and hidden minerals unconquered fastnesses that might, it seemed, hold out for centuries before they gave their treasure. How quickly things had come! "Progress, progress," murmured the wheels, and I began to make this steady, swift, and shiningly equipped train a figure, just as I had made the *Carmania* a figure of that big onward sweep that is moving us all together. It was not a noisy train, after the English fashion, nor did the cars sway and jump after the habit of our lighter coaches, but the air was full of deep, triumphant rhythms. "It goes on," I said, "invincibly," and even as the thought was in my head, the brakes set up a droning, a vibration ran through the train and we slowed and stopped. A minute passed, and then we rumbled softly back to a little trestle-bridge and stood there.

I got up, looked from the window, and then went to the platform at the end of the train. I found two men, a passenger and a colored parlor-car attendant. The former was on the bottom step of the car, the latter was supplying him with information.

"His head's still in the water," he remarked.

"Whose head?" said I.

"A man we've killed," said he. "We caught him in the trestle-bridge."

I descended a step, craned over my fellow-passenger, and saw a little group standing curiously about the derelict thing that had been a living man three minutes before. It was now a crumpled, dark-stained blue blouse, a limply broken arm with hand askew, trousered legs that sprawled quaintly, and a pair of heavy boots, lying in the sunlit fresh grass by the water below the trestle-bridge. . . .

A man on the line gave inadequate explanations. "He'd have been all right if he hadn't come over this side," he said.

"Who was he?" said I.

"One of these Eyetalians on the line," he said, and turned away. The train bristled now with a bunch of curiosity at every car end, and even windows were opened. . . .

Presently it was intimated to us by a whistle and the hasty return of men to the cars that the incident had closed. We began to move forward again, crept up to speed. . . .

But I could not go on with my conception of the train as a symbol of human advancement. That crumpled blue blouse and queerly careless legs would get into the picture and set up all sorts of alien speculations. I thought of distant north Italian valleys and brown boys among the vines and goats, of the immigrants who had sung remotely to me out of the *Carmania's* steerage, of the hopeful bright-eyed procession of the new-comers through Ellis Island wicket, of the regiments of workers the line had shown me, and I told myself a tale of this Italian's journey to the land of promise, this land of gigantic promises. . . .

For a time the big spectacle of America about me took on a quality of magnificent infidelity. . . .

And by reason of this incident my last Image of Material Progress thundered into Washington station five minutes behind its scheduled time.

CHAPTER V

THE ECONOMIC PROCESS

I

LET me try now and make some sort
A Bird's-Eye View of general picture of the American
nation as it impresses itself upon me.
It is, you will understand, the vision of a hurried
bird of passage, defective and inaccurate at every
point of detail, but perhaps for my present purpose
not so very much the worse for that. The fact that I
am transitory and bring a sort of theorizing naïveté
to this review is just what gives me the chance to re-
mark these obvious things the habituated have forgotten. I have already tried to render something
of the effect of huge unrestrained growth and material progress that America first gives one, and I
have pointed out that so far America seems to me
only to refresh an old impression, to give starkly
and startlingly what is going on everywhere, what
is indeed as much in evidence in Birkenhead or
Milan or London or Calcutta, a huge extension
of human power and the scale of human operations. This growth was elaborated in the physical

and chemical laboratories and the industrial experiments of the eighteenth and early nineteenth century, and chiefly in Europe. The extension itself is nothing typically American. Nevertheless America now shows it best. America is most under the stress and urgency of it, resonates most readily and loudly to its note.

The long distances of travel, and the sense of isolation between place and place, the remoteness verging upon inaudibility of Washington in Chicago, of Chicago in Boston, the vision I have had of America from observation cars and railroad windows brings home to me more and more that this huge development of human appliances and resources is here going on in a community that is still, for all the dense crowds of New York, the teeming congestion of the East Side, extraordinarily scattered. America, one recalls, is still an unoccupied country, across which the latest developments of civilization are rushing. We are dealing here with a continuous area of land which is, leaving Alaska out of account altogether, equal to Great Britain, France, the German Empire, the Austro-Hungarian Empire, Italy, Belgium, Japan, Holland, Spain and Portugal, Sweden and Norway, Turkey in Europe, Egypt and the whole Empire of India, and the population spread out over this vast space is still less than the joint population of the first two countries named and not a quarter that of India. Moreover, it is not spread at all evenly. Much of it is in undistributed clots. It is not upon the soil, barely half of it is in holdings and homes and authentic communities. It is a population of an extremely modern type. Urban concentration has already gone far with it; fifteen millions of it are crowded into and about twenty great cities, other eighteen millions make up five hundred towns. Between these centres of population run railways indeed, telegraph wires, telephone connections, tracks of various sorts, but to the European eye these are mere scratchings on a virgin surface. An empty wilderness manifests itself through this thin network of human conveniences, appears in the meshes even at the railroad side. Essentially America is still an unsettled land, with only a few incidental good roads in favored places, with no universal police, with no wayside inns where a civilized man may rest, with still only the crudest of rural postal deliveries, with long stretches of swamp and forest and desert by the track side, still unassailed by industry. This much one sees clearly enough eastward of Chicago. Westward, I am told, it becomes more and more the fact. In Idaho at last, comes the untouched and perhaps invincible desert, plain and continuous through the long hours of travel. Huge areas do not contain one human being to the square mile, still vaster portions fall short of two. . . .

And this community, to which material progress is bringing such enormous powers, and that is knotted so densely here and there, and is otherwise so attenuated a veil over the huge land surface, is, as Professor Münsterberg points out, in spite of vast and increasing masses of immigrants still a curiously homogeneous one, homogeneous in the spirit of its activities and speaking a common tongue. It is sustained by certain economic conventions, inspired throughout by certain habits, certain trends of suggestion, certain phrases and certain interpretations that collectively make up what one may call the American Idea. To the process of enlargement and diffusion and increase and multiplying resources, we must now bring the consideration of the social and economic process that is going on. What is the form of that process as one finds it in America? An English Tory will tell you promptly, "a scramble for dollars." A good American will tell you it is self realization under equality of opportunity. The English Tory will probably allege that that amounts to the same thing.

Let us look into that.

II

ONE contrast between America and
Liberty of the old world I had in mind before
Property ever I crossed the Atlantic, and now it comes before me very vividly,—returns reinforced by a hundred little things observed and felt. The contrast consists in the almost complete absence

6   71

from the normal American scheme, of certain im-
memorial factors in the social structure of our
European nations.

In the first place, every European nation except
the English is rooted to the soil by a peasantry, and
even in England one still finds the peasant repre-
sented, in most of his features by those sons of dis-
possessed serf - peasants, the agricultural laborers.
Here in America, except in the regions where the
negro abounds, there is no lower stratum, no "soil
people," to this community at all; your bottom-
most man is a mobile free man who can read, and
who has ideas above digging and pigs and poultry
keeping, except incidentally for his own ends. No
one owns to subordination. As a consequence, any
position which involves the acknowledgment of an
innate inferiority is difficult to fill; there is, from
the European point of view, an extraordinary
dearth of servants, and this endures in spite of a
great peasant immigration. The servile tradition
will not root here now, it dies in this soil. An
enormous importation of European serfs and peasants goes on, but as they touch this soil their backs
begin to stiffen with a new assertion.

And at the other end of the scale, also, one misses
an element. There is no territorial aristocracy, no
aristocracy at all, no throne, no legitimate and acknowledged representative of that upper social
structure of leisure, power, State responsibility,
which in the old European theory of society was

supposed to give significance to the whole. The American community, one cannot too clearly insist, does not correspond to an entire European community at all, but only to the middle masses of it, to the trading and manufacturing class between the dimensions of the magnate and the clerk and skilled artisan. It is the central part of the European organism without either the dreaming head or the subjugated feet. Even the highly feudal slave-holding "county family" traditions of Virginia and the South pass now out of memory. So that in a very real sense the past of this American community is in Europe, and the settled order of the past is left behind there. This community was, as it were, taken off its roots, clipped of its branches and brought hither. It began neither serf nor lord, but burgher and farmer, it followed the normal development of the middle class under Progress everywhere and became capitalistic. Essentially America is a middle-class become a community and so its essential problems are the problems of a modern individualistic society, stark and clear, unhampered and unilluminated by any feudal traditions either at its crest or at its base.

It would be interesting and at first only very slightly misleading to pursue the rough contrast of American and English conditions upon these lines. It is not difficult to show for example, that the two great political parties in America represent only one English party, the middle-class Liberal party,

the party of industrialism and freedom. There are
no Tories to represent the feudal system, and no
Labor party. It is history, it is no mere ingenious
gloss upon history, that the Tories, the party of the
crown, of the high gentry and control, of mitigated
property and an organic state, vanished from
America at the Revolution. They left the new
world to the Whigs and Nonconformists and to
those less constructive, less logical, more popular
and liberating thinkers who became Radicals in
England, and Jeffersonians and then Democrats in
America. All Americans are, from the English
point of view, Liberals of one sort or another. You
will find a fac-simile of the Declaration of Independence displayed conspicuously and triumphantly beside Magna Charter in the London Reform Club, to carry out this suggestion.

But these fascinating parallelisms will lead away
from the chief argument in hand, which is that the
Americans started almost clear of the medieval
heritage, and developed in the utmost—purity if
you like — or simplicity or crudeness, whichever
you will, the modern type of productive social
organization. They took the economic conventions that were modern and progressive at the
end of the eighteenth century and stamped them
into the Constitution as if they meant to stamp
them there for all time. In England you can still
find feudalism, medievalism, the Renascence, at
every turn. America is pure eighteenth century

—still crystallizing out from a turbid and troubled solution.

To turn from any European state to America is, in these matters anyhow, to turn from complication to a stark simplicity. The relationship between employer and employed, between organizer and worker, between capital and labor, which in England is qualified and mellowed and disguised and entangled with a thousand traditional attitudes and subordinations, stands out sharply in a bleak cold rationalism. There is no feeling that property, privilege, honor, and a grave liability to official public service ought to go together, none that uncritical obedience is a virtue in a worker or that subordination carries with it not only a sense of service but a claim for help. Coming across the Atlantic has in these matters an effect of coming out of an iridescent fog into a clear bright air.

This homologization of the whole American social mass, not with the whole English social mass, but with its "modern" classes, its great middle portion, and of its political sides with the two ingredients of English Liberalism, goes further than a rough parallel. An Englishman who, like myself, has been bred and who has lived all his life either in London, with its predominant West-End, or the southern counties with their fair large estates and the great country houses, is constantly being reminded, when he meets manufacturing and business men from Birmingham or Lancashire, of Americans, and when he meets Americans, of industrial North-country people. There is more push and less tacit assumption, more definition, more displayed energy and less restraint, more action and less subtlety, more enterprise and self-assertion than there is in the typical Englishman of London and the home counties. The American carries on the contrast further, it is true, and his speech is not northernly, but marked by the accent of Hampshire or East Anglia, and better and clearer than his English equivalent's; but one feels the two are of the same stuff, nevertheless, and made by parallel conditions. The liberalism of the eighteenth century, the material progress of the nineteenth have made them both—out of the undifferentiated Stuart Englishman. And they are the same in their attitude towards property and social duty, individualists to the marrow. But the one grew inside a frame of regal, aristocratic, and feudal institutions, and has chafed against it, struggled with it, modified it, strained it, and been modified by it, but has remained within it; the other broke it and escaped to complete self-development.

The liberalism of the eighteenth century was essentially the rebellion of the modern industrial organization against the monarchial and aristocratic State,—against hereditary privilege, against restrictions upon bargains—whether they were hard bargains or not. Its spirit was essentially Anarchistic, —the antithesis of Socialism. It was the anti-State.

It aimed not only to liberate men but property from State control. Its most typical expressions, the Declaration of Independence, and the French Declaration of the Rights of Man, are zealously emphatic for the latter interest—for the sacredness of contracts and possessions. Post Reformation liberalism did to a large extent let loose property upon mankind. The English Civil War of the seventeenth century, like the American revolution of the eighteenth, embodied essentially the triumphant refusal of private property to submit to taxation without consent. In England the result was tempered and qualified, security for private property was achieved, but not cast-iron security; each man who had property became king of that property, but only a constitutional and conditional king. In America the victory of private property was complete. Let one instance suffice to show how decisively it was established that individual property and credit and money were sacred. Ten years ago the Supreme Court, trying a case arising out of the General Revenue tax of 1894, decided that a graduated income-tax, such as the English Parliament might pass to-morrow, can never be levied upon the United States nation without a change in the Constitution, which can be effected only by a vote of two-thirds of both Houses of Congress as an initiative, and this must be ratified either by the legislatures of three-fourths of the States, or by special conventions representing three-fourths of the States

The fundamental law of the States forbids any such invasion of the individual's ownership. No national income-tax is legal, and there is practically no power, short of revolution, to alter that. . . .

Could anything be more emphatic? That tall Liberty with its spiky crown that stands in New York Harbor and casts an electric flare upon the world, is, indeed, the liberty of Property, and there she stands at the Zenith. . . .

III

Aggregation and Some Protests   Now the middle-class of the English population and the whole population of America that matters at all when we discuss ideas, is essentially an emancipated class, a class that has rebelled against superimposed privilege and honor, and achieved freedom for its individuals and their property. Without property its freedom is a featureless and unsubstantial theory, and so it relies for the reality of life upon that, upon the possession and acquisition and development of property, that is to say upon "business." That is the quality of its life.

Everywhere in the modern industrial and commercial class this deep-lying feeling that the State is something escaped from, has worked out to the same mental habit of social irresponsibility, and in America it has worked unimpeded. Patriotism has become a mere national self - assertion, a sentimentality of flag cheering, with no constructive duties. Law, social justice, the pride and preservation of the state as a whole are taken as provided for before the game began, and one devotes oneself to business. At business all men are held to be equal, and none is his brother's keeper.

All men are equal at the great game of business. You try for the best of each bargain and so does your opponent; if you chance to have more in your hand than he—well, that's *your* advantage, and you use it. Presently he may have more than you. You take care he doesn't if you can, but you play fair—except for the advantage in your hand; you play fair—and hard.

Now this middle - class equality ultimately destroys itself. Out of this conflict of equals, and by virtue of the fact that property, like all sorts of matter, does tend to gravitate towards itself whenever it is free, there emerge the modern rich and the modern toiler.

One can trace the process in two or three generations in Lancashire or the Potteries, or any industrial region of England. One sees first the early Lancashire industrialism, sees a district of cotton-spinners more or less equal together, small men all; then come developments, comes a state of ideally free competition with some men growing large, with most men dropping into employment, but still with ample chances for an industrious young man to

end as a prosperous master; and so through a
steady growth in the size of the organization to the
present opposition of an employer class in possession of everything, almost inaccessibly above, and
an employed class below. The railways come, and
the wealthy class reaches out to master these new
enterprises, capitalistic from the outset. . . .

America is simply repeating the history of the
Lancashire industrialism on a gigantic scale, and
under an enormous variety of forms.

But in England, as the modern Rich rise up, they
come into a world of gentry with a tradition of
public service and authority; they learn one by one
and assimilate themselves to the legend of the
"governing class" with a sense of proprietorship
which is also, in its humanly limited way, a sense
of duty to the state. They are pseudomorphs after
aristocrats. They receive honors, they inter-marry,
they fall (and their defeated competitors too fall)
into the mellowed relationships of an aristocratic
system. That is not a permanent mutual attitude;
it does, however, mask and soften the British out-
line. Industrialism becomes quasi-feudal. America,
on the other hand, had no effectual "governing
class," there has been no such modification, no
clouding of the issue. Its Rich, to one's superficial
inspection, do seem to lop out, swell up into an immense consumption and power and inanity, develop no sense of public duties, remain winners of a
strange game they do not criticise, concerned now

only to hold and intensify their winnings. The losers accept no subservience. That material progress, that secular growth in scale of all modern enterprises, widens the gulf between Owner and Worker daily. More and more do men realize that this game of free competition and unrestricted property does not go on for ever; it is a game that first in this industry and then in that, and at last in all, can be played out and is being played out. Property becomes organized, consolidated, concentrated, and secured. This is the fact to which America is slowly awaking at the present time. The American community is discovering a secular extinction of opportunity, and the appearance of powers against which individual enterprise and competition are hopeless. Enormous sections of the American public are losing their faith in any personal chance of growing rich and truly free, and are developing the consciousness of an expropriated class.

This realization has come slowlier in America than in Europe, because of the enormous undeveloped resources of America. So long as there was an unlimited extent of unappropriated and unexplored land westward, so long could tension be relieved by so simple an injunction as Horace Greeley's, "Go West, young man; go West." And to-day, albeit that is no longer true of the land, and there are already far larger concentrations of individual possessions in the United States of

America than anywhere else in the world, yet so vast are their continental resources that it still remains true that nowhere in the world is property so widely diffused. Consider the one fact that America can take in three-quarters of a million of workers in one year without producing a perceptible fall in wages, and you will appreciate the scale upon which things are measured here, the scale by which even Mr. J. D. Rockefeller's billion dollars becomes no more than a respectable but by no means overwhelming "pile." For all these concentrations, the western farmers still own their farms, and it is the rule rather than the exception for a family to possess the freehold of the house it lives in. But the process of concentration goes on nevertheless—is going on now perceptibly to the American mind. That it has not gone so far as in the European instance it is a question of size, just as the gestation of an elephant takes longer than that of a mouse. If the process is larger and slower, it is, for the reasons I have given, plainer, and it will be discussed and dealt with plainly. That steady trend towards concentration under individualistic rules, until individual competition becomes disheartened and hopeless, is the essential form of the economic and social process in America as I see it now, and it has become the cardinal topic of thought and discussion in the American mind.

This realization has been reached after the most curious hesitation. There is every reason for this;

WESTERN FARMERS STILL OWN THEIR FARMS

for it involves the contradiction of much that seems fundamental in the American idea. It amounts to a national change of attitude. It is a conscious change of attitude that is being deliberately made.

This slow reluctant process of disillusionment with individualism is interestingly traceable through the main political innovations of the last twenty years. There was the discovery in the east that the supply of land was not limitless, and we had the Single Tax movement, and the epoch of the first Mr. Henry George. He explained fervently of course, how individualistic, how profoundly American he was—but land was not to be monopolized. Then came the discovery in the west that there were limits to borrowing and that gold appreciated against the debtor, and so we have the Populist movement and extraordinary schemes for destroying the monopolization of gold and credit. Mr. Bryan led that and nearly captured the country, but only in last May's issue of the *Century Magazine* I found him explaining (expounding meanwhile a largely socialistic programme) that he too is an Individualist of the purest water. And then the attack shifted to the destruction of free competition by the trusts. The small business went on sufferance, not knowing from week to week when its hour to sell out or fight might come. The Trusts have crushed competition, raised prices against the consumer, and served him often quite abominably. The curious reader may find in Mr. Upton Sinclair's essentially veracious *Jungle* the possibilities of individualistic enterprise in the matter of food and decency. The States have been agitated by a big disorganized Anti-Trust movement for some years, it becomes of the gravest political importance at every election, and the sustained study of the affairs and methods of that most typical and prominent of trust organizations, the Standard Oil Company, by Miss Tarbell and a host of followers, is bringing to light more and more clearly the defencelessness of the common person, and his hopelessness, however enterprising, as a competitor against those great business aggregations. His faith in all his reliances and securities fades in the new light that grows about him, he sees his little investments, his insurance policy, his once open and impartial route to market by steamboat and rail, all passing into the grip of the great property accumulators. The aggregation of property has created powers that are stronger than state legislatures and more persistent than any public opinion can be, that have no awe and no sentiment for legislation, that are prepared to disregard it or evade it whenever they can.

And these aggregations are taking on immortality and declining to disintegrate when their founders die. The Astor property, the Jay Gould property, the Marshall Field property, for example, do not break up, become undying centres for the concentration of wealth, and it is doubtful if there is any power to hinder such a development of perpetual fortunes. In England when Thelussen left his investments to accumulate, a simple little act of Parliament set his will aside. But Congress is not sovereign, there is no national sovereign power in America, and Property in America, it would seem, is absolutely free to do these things. So you have President Roosevelt in a recent oration attacking the man with the Muck Rake (who gathered vile dross for the love of it), and threatening the limitation of inheritance. But he too, quite as much as Mr. Bryan, assures the public that he is a fervent individualist.

So in this American community, whose distinctive conception is its emphatic assertion of the freedom of individual property, whose very symbol is that spike-crowned Liberty gripping a torch in New York Harbor, there has been and is going on a successive repudiation of that freedom in almost every department of ownable things by considerable masses of thinking people, a denial of the soundness of individual property in land, an organized attempt against the accumulation of gold and credit, by a systematic watering of the currency, a revolt against the aggregatory outcome of untrammelled business competition, a systematic interference with the freedom of railways and carriers to do business as they please, and a protest from the most representative of Americans against hereditary wealth. . . .

That, in general terms, is the economic and social process as one sees it in America now, a process of systematically concentrating wealth on the part of an energetic minority, and of a great insurgence of alarm, of waves of indignation and protest and threat on the part of that vague indefinite public that Mr. Roosevelt calls the "nation."

And this goes on side by side with a process of material progress that partly masks its quality, that keeps the standard of life from falling and prevents any sense of impoverishment among the mass of the losers in the economic struggle. Through this material progress there is a constant substitution of larger, cleaner, more efficient possibilities, and more and more wholesale and far-sighted methods of organization for the dark, confused, untidy individualistic expedients of the Victorian time. An epoch which was coaly and mechanical, commercial and adventurous after the earlier fashion is giving place, almost automatically, to one that will be electrical and scientific, artistic and creative. The material progress due to a secular increase in knowledge, and the economic progress interfere and combine with and complicate one another, the former constantly changes the forms and appliances of the latter, changes the weapons and conditions, and may ultimately change the spirit and conceptions of the struggle. The latter now clogs and arrests the former. So in its broad features, as a conflict between the birth strength of a splendid civilization and a hampering commercialism, I see America.

CHAPTER VI

SOME ASPECTS OF AMERICAN WEALTH

I

IT is obvious that in a community
The Spenders that has disavowed aristocracy or rule
and subordination or service, which
has granted unparalleled freedoms to property and
despised and distrusted the state, the chief business
of life will consist in getting or attempting to get.
But the chief aspect of American life that impinges
first upon the European is not this, but the be-
havior of a certain overflow at the top, of people
who have largely and triumphantly got, and with
hand, pockets, safe-deposit vaults full of dollars,
are proceeding to realize victory. Before I came to
America it was in his capacity of spender that I
chiefly knew the American; as a person who had
demoralized Regent Street and the Rue de Rivoli,
who had taught the London cabman to demand
"arf a dollar" for a shilling fare, who bought old
books and old castles, and had driven the prices
of old furniture to incredible altitudes, and was
slowly transferring our incubus of artistic achieve-

ment to American soil. One of my friends in London is Mr. X, who owns those two houses full of fine "pieces" near the British Museum and keeps his honor unsullied in the most deleterious of trades. "They come to me," he said, "and ask me to buy for them. It's just buying. One of them wants to beat the silver of another, doesn't care what he pays. Another clamors for tapestry. They trust me as they trust a doctor. There's no understanding—no feeling. It's hard to treat them well."

And there is the story of Y, who is wise about pictures. "If you want a Botticelli that size, Mr. Record, I can't find it," he said; "you'll have to have it made for you."

These American spenders have got the whole world "beat" at the foolish game of collecting, and in all the peculiar delights of shopping they excel. And they are the crown and glory of hotel managers throughout the world. There is something naïve, something childishly expectant and acquisitive, about this aspect of American riches. There appears no aristocracy in their tradition, no sense of permanence and great responsibility, there appears no sense of subordination and service; from the individualistic business struggle they have emerged triumphant, and what is there to do now but spend and have a good time?

They swarm in the pleasant places of the Riviera, they pervade Paris and Rome, they occupy Scotch castles and English estates, their motor-cars are terrible and wonderful. And the London Savoy Hotel still flaunts its memory of one splendid American night. The court-yard was flooded with water tinted an artistic blue—to the great discomfort of the practically inevitable gold-fish, and on this floated a dream of a gondola. And in the gondola the table was spread and served by the Savoy staff, mysteriously disguised in appropriate fancy costume. The whole thing—there's only two words for it—was "perfectly lovely." "The illusion"— whatever that was—we are assured, was complete. It wasn't a nursery treat, you know. The guests, I am told, were important grown-up people.

This sort of childishness, of course, has nothing distinctively American in it. Any people of sluggish and uneducated imagination who find themselves profusely wealthy, and are too stupid to understand the huge moral burden, the burden of splendid possibilities it carries, may do things of this sort. It was not Americans but a party of South-African millionaires who achieved the kindred triumph of the shirt-and-belt dinner under a tent in a London hotel dining-room. The glittering procession of carriages and motor-carriages which I watched driving down Fifth Avenue, New York, apparently for the pleasure of driving up again, is to be paralleled on the Pincio, in Naples, in Paris, and anywhere where irresponsible pleasure-seekers gather together. After the naïve joy of buying

PLUMP AND PRETTY PUPILS OF EXTRAVAGANCE

things comes the joy of wearing them publicly, the simple pleasure of the promenade. These things are universals. But nowhere has this spending struck me as being so solid and substantial, so nearly twenty-two carats fine, as here. The shops have an air of solid worth, are in the key of butlers, bishops, opera-boxes, high-class florists, powdered footmen, Roman beadles, motor-broughams, to an extent that altogether outshines either Paris or London.

And in such great hotels as the Waldorf-Astoria, one finds the new arrivals, the wives and daughters from the West and the South, in new, bright hats, and splendors of costume, clubbed together, under the discreetest management, for this and that, learning how to spend collectively, reaching out to assemblies, to dinners. From an observant tea-table beneath the fronds of a palm, I surveyed a fine array of these plump and pretty pupils of extravagance. They were for the most part quite brilliantly as well as newly dressed, and with an artless and pleasing unconsciousness of the living from inside. Smart innocents! I found all that gathering most contagiously interested and happy and fresh.

And I watched spending, too, as one sees it in the various incompatible houses of upper Fifth Avenue and along the border of Central Park. That, too, suggests a shop, a shop where country houses are sold and stored; there is the Tiffany house, a most expensive - looking article, on the shelf, and the Carnegie house. There had been no pretence on the part of the architects that any house belonged in any sense to any other, that any sort of community held them together. The link is just spending. You come to New York and spend; you go away again. To some of these palaces people came and went; others had their blinds down and conveyed a curious effect of a sunlit child excursionist in a train who falls asleep and droops against his neighbor. One of the Vanderbilt houses was frankly and brutally boarded up. Newport, I am told, takes up and carries on the same note of magnificent irresponsibility, and there one admires the richest forms of simplicity, triumphs of villa architecture in thatch, and bathing bungalows in marble. . . .

There exists already, of these irresponsible American rich, a splendid group of portraits, done without extenuation and without malice, in the later work of that great master of English fiction, Mr. Henry James. There one sees them at their best, their refinement, their large wealthiness, their incredible unreality. I think of *The Ambassadors* and that mysterious source of the income of the Newcomes, a mystery that, with infinite artistic tact, was never explained; but more I think of *The Golden Bowl*, most spacious and serene of novels.

In that splendid and luminous bubble, the Prince Amerigo and Maggie Verver, Mr. Verver, that assiduous collector, and the adventurous Charlotte Stant float far above a world of toil and anxiety, spending with a large refinement, with a perfected assurance and precision. They spend as flowers open. But this is the quintessence, the sublimation, the idealization of the rich American. Few have the restraint for this. For the rest, when one has shopped and shopped, and collected and bought everything, and promenaded on foot, in motor-car and motor-brougham and motor-boat, in yacht and special train; when one has a fine house here and a fine house there, and photography and the special article have exhausted admiration, there remains chiefly that one broader and more presumptuous pleasure—spending to give. American givers give most generously, and some of them, it must be admitted, give well. But they give individually, incoherently, each pursuing a personal ideal. There are unsuccessful givers. . . .

American cities are being littered with a disorder of unsystematized foundations and picturesque legacies, much as I find my nursery floor littered with abandoned toys and battles and buildings when the children are in bed after a long, wet day. Yet some of the gifts are very splendid things. There is, for example, the Leland Stanford Junior University in California, a vast monument of parental affection and Richardsonian architecture, with professors, and teaching going on in its interstices; and there is Mrs. Gardner's delightful

Fenway Court, a Venetian palace, brought almost bodily from Italy and full of finely gathered treasures. . . .

All this giving is, in its aggregate effect, as confused as industrial Chicago. It presents no clear scheme of the future, promises no growth; it is due to the impulsive generosity of a mob of wealthy persons, with no broad common conceptions, with no collective dream, with little to hold them together but imitation and the burning possession of money; the gifts overlap, they lie at any angle, one with another. Some are needless, some mischievous. There are great gaps of unfulfilled need between.

And through the multitude of lesser, though still mighty, givers, comes that colossus of property, Mr. Andrew Carnegie, the jubilee plunger of beneficence, that rosy, gray-haired, nimble little figure, going to and fro between two continents, scattering library buildings as if he sowed wild oats, buildings that may or may not have some educational value, if presently they are reorganized and properly stocked with books. Anon he appals the thrifty burgesses of Dunfermline with vast and uncongenial responsibilities of expenditure; anon he precipitates the library of the late Lord Acton upon our embarrassed Mr. Morley; anon he pauperizes the students of Scotland. He diffuses his monument throughout the English-speaking lands, amid circumstances of the most flagrant publicity; the receptive learned, the philanthropic noble, bow in expectant swaths before him. He is the American fable come true; nothing seems too wild to believe of him, and he fills the European imagination with an altogether erroneous conception of the self-dissipating quality in American wealth.

II

BECAUSE, now, as a matter of fact, dissipation is by no means the characteristic quality of American getting. The good American will indeed tell you solemnly that in America it is three generations "from shirt-sleeves to shirt-sleeves"; but this has about as much truth in it as that remarkable absence of any pure-bred Londoners of the third generation, dear to the British imagination.

The Astor Fortune

Amid the vast yeasty tumult of American business, of the getting and losing which are the main life of this community, nothing could be clearer than the steady accumulation of great masses of property that show no signs of disintegrating again. The very rich people display an indisposition to divide their estates; the Marshall Field estate in Chicago, for example, accumulates; the Jay Gould inheritance survives great strains. And when first I heard that "shirt-sleeves to shirt-sleeves" proverb, which is so fortifying a consolation to the older school of Americans, my mind flew back to the Thames Embankment, as one sees it from the steamboat on the river. There, just eastward of the tall red Education offices of the London County Council, stands a quite graceful and decorative little building of gray stone, that jars not at all with the fine traditions of the adjacent Temple, but catches the eye, nevertheless, with its very big, very gilded vane in the form of a ship. This is the handsome strong-box to which New York pays gigantic yearly tribute, the office in which Mr. W. W. Astor conducts his affairs. They are not his private and individual affairs, but the affairs of the estate of the late J. J. Astor—still undivided, and still growing year by year.

Mr. Astor seems to me to be a much more representative figure of American wealth than any of the conspicuous spenders who strike so vividly upon the European imagination. His is the most retiring of personalities. In this picturesque stone casket he works; his staff works under his cognizance, and administers, I know not to what ends nor to what extent, revenues that exceed those of many sovereign states. He himself is impressed by it, and, without arrogance, he makes a visit to his offices, with a view of its storage vaults, its halls of disciplined clerks, a novel and characteristic form of entertainment. For the rest, Mr. Astor leads a life of modest affluence, and recreates himself with the genealogy of his family, short stories about treasure lost and found, and such like literary work.

Now here you have wealth with, as it were, the minimum of ownership, as indeed owning its possessor. Nobody seems to be spending that huge income the crowded enormity of New York squeezes out. The "Estate of the late J. J. Astor" must be accumulating more wealth and still more; under careful and systematic management must be rolling up like a golden snowball under that golden weather-vane. In the most accidental relation to its undistinguished, harmless, arithmetical proprietor!

Your anarchist orator or your crude socialist is always talking of the rich as blood-suckers, robbers, robber-barons, *grafters* and so on. It really is nonsense to talk like that. In the presence of Mr. W. W. Astor these preposterous accusations answer themselves. The thing is a logical outcome of the assumptions about private property on which our contemporary civilization is based, and Mr. Astor, for all that he draws gold from New York as effectually as a ferret draws blood from a rabbit, is indeed the most innocent of men. He finds himself in a certain position, and he sits down very congenially and adds and adds and adds, and relieves the tedium of his leisure in literary composition. Had he been born at the level of a dry-goods clerk he would probably have done the same sort of thing on a smaller scale, and it would have been the little Poddlecombe literary society, and not the *Pall Mall Magazine*, that would have been the richer for his compositions. It is just the scale of the circumstances that differs. . . .

III

The Chief
Getters THE lavish spending of Fifth Avenue and Paris and Rome and Mayfair is but the flower, the often brilliant, the sometimes gaudy flower of the American economic process; and such slow and patient accumulators as Mr. Astor the rounding and ripening fruit. One need be only a little while in America to realize this, and to discern the branch and leaf, and at last even the aggressive insatiable spreading root of aggregating property, that was liberated so effectually when America declared herself free.

The group of people that attracts the largest amount of attention in press and talk, that most obsesses the American imagination, and that is indeed the most significant at the present time, is the little group — a few score men perhaps altogether — who are emerging distinctly as winners in that great struggle to get, into which this commercial industrialism has naturally resolved itself. Central among them are the men of the Standard Oil group, the "octopus" which spreads its ramifying tentacles through the whole system of American business, absorbing and absorbing, grasping and growing. The extraordinarily able investigations of such writers as Miss Tarbell and Ray Stannard Baker, the rhetorical exposures of Mr. T. W. Lawson, have brought out the methods and quality of this group of persons with a particularity that has been reserved heretofore for great statesmen and crowned heads, and with an unflattering lucidity altogether unprecedented. Not only is every hair on their heads numbered, but the number is published. They are known to their pettiest weaknesses and to their most accidental associations. And in this astonishing blaze of illumination they continue steadfastly to get.

These men, who are creating the greatest system of correlated private properties in the world, who are wealthy beyond all precedent, seem for the most part to be men with no ulterior dream or aim. They are not voluptuaries, they are neither artists nor any sort of creators, and they betray no high political ambitions. Had they anything of the sort they would not be what. they are, they would be more than that and less. They want and they get, they are inspired by the brute will in their wealth to have more wealth and moɹe, to a systematic ardor. They are men of a competing, patient, enterprising, acquisitive enthusiasm. They have found in America the perfectly favorable environment for their temperaments. In no other country and in no other age could they have risen to such eminence. America is still, by virtue of its great Puritan tradition and in the older sense of the word, an intensely moral land. Most lusts here are strongly curbed, by public opinion, by training and tradition. But the lust of acquisition has not been curbed but glorified. . . .

These financial leaders are accused by the press of every sort of crime in the development of their great organizations and their fight against competitors, but I feel impelled myself to acquit them of anything so heroic as a general scheme of criminality, as a systematic organization of power. They are men with a good deal of contempt for legislation and state interference, but that is no distinction, it has unhappily been part of the training of the average American citizen, and they have no doubt exceeded the letter if not the spirit of the laws of business competition. They have played to win and not for style, and if they personally had not done so somebody else would; they fill a position which from the nature of things, somebody is bound to fill. They have, no doubt, carried sharpness to the very edge of dishonesty, but what else was to be expected from the American conditions? Only by doing so and taking risks is pre-eminent success in getting to be attained. They have developed an enormous system of espionage, but on his smaller scale every retail grocer, every employer of servants does something in that way. They have secret agents, false names, con-

cealed bargains, — what else could one expect?
People have committed suicide through their
operations — but in a game which is bound to
bring the losers to despair it is childish to charge
the winners with murder. It's the game that is
criminal. It is ridiculous, I say, to write of these
men as though they were unparalleled villains, intellectual overmen, conscienceless conquerors of the
world. Mr. J. D. Rockefeller's mild, thin - lipped,
pleasant face gives the lie to all such melo-
dramatic nonsense.

I must confess to a sneaking liking for this much-
reviled man. One thinks of Miss Tarbell's description of him, displaying his first boyish account-
book, his ledger A, to a sympathetic gathering of
the Baptist young, telling how he earned fifty dollars in the first three months of his clerking in a
Chicago warehouse, and how savingly he dealt with
it. Hear his words:

"You could not get that book from me for all the
modern ledgers in New York, nor for all that they
would bring. It almost brings tears to my eyes
when I read over this little book, and it fills me
with a sense of gratitude I cannot express. . . .

"I know some people, . . . especially some young
men, find it difficult to keep a little money in their
pocket-book. I learned to keep money, and, as we
have a way of saying, it did not burn a hole in my
pocket. I was taught that it was the thing to keep
the money and take care of it. Among the early

experiences that were helpful to me that I recollect
with pleasure, was one of working a few days for
a neighbor digging potatoes—an enterprising and
thrifty farmer who could dig a great many potatoes. I was a boy perhaps thirteen or fourteen
years of age, and he kept me busy from morning
until night. It was a ten-hour day. . . .

"And as I was saving these little sums, I soon
learned I could get as much interest for fifty dollars
loaned at seven per cent.—the legal rate in the
State of New York at that time for a year—as I
could earn by digging potatoes ten days. The impression was gaining ground with me that it was a
good thing to let money be my slave and not make
myself a slave to money. I have tried to remember
that in every sense."

This is not the voice of any sort of contemptuous
trampler of his species. This is the voice of an industrious, acquisitive, commonplace, pious man, as
honestly and simply proud of his acquisitiveness as
a stamp-collector might be. At times, in his ac-
quisitions, the strength of his passion may have
driven him to lengths beyond the severe moral code,
but the same has been true of stamp-collectors.
He is a man who has taken up with great natural
aptitude an ignoble tradition which links economy
and earning with piety and honor. His teachers
were to blame, that Baptist community that is
now so ashamed of its son that it refuses his gifts.
To a large extent he is the creature of opportunity;

he has been flung to the topmost pinnacle of human envy, partly by accident, partly by that peculiarity of American conditions that has subordinated, in the name of liberty, all the grave and ennobling affairs of statecraft to a middle-class freedom of commercial enterprise. Quarrel with that if you like. It is unfair and ridiculous to quarrel with him.

CHAPTER VII

CERTAIN WORKERS

I

LET us now look a little at another aspect of this process of individualistic competition which is the economic process in America, and which is giving us on its upper side the spenders of Fifth Avenue, the slow accumulators of the Astor type, and the great getters of the giant business organizations, the Trusts and acquisitive finance. We have concluded that this process of free and open competition in business which, clearly, the framers of the American Constitution imagined to be immortal, does as a matter of fact tend to kill itself through the advantage property gives in the acquisition of more property. But before we can go on to estimate the further future of this process we must experiment with another question. What is happening to those who have not got and who are not getting wealth, who are, in fact, falling back in the competition?

Now there can be little doubt to any one who

goes to and fro in America that in spite of the huge accumulation of property in a few hands that is now in progress, there is still no general effect of impoverishment. To me, coming from London to New York, the effect of the crowd in the trolley-cars and subways and streets was one of exceptional prosperity. New York has no doubt its effects of noise, disorder, discomfort, and a sort of brutality, but to begin with one sees nothing of the underfed people, the numerous dingily clad and grayly housed people who catch the eye in London. Even in the congested arteries, the filthy back streets of the East Side I found myself saying, as a thing re-markable, "These people have money to spend." In London one travels long distances for two cents, and great regiments of people walk; in New York the universal fare is five cents and everybody rides. Common people are better gloved and better booted in America than in any European country I know, in spite of the higher prices for clothing here, the men wear ready-made suits, it is true, to a much greater extent, but they are newer and brighter than the London clerk's carefully brushed, tailor-made garments. Wages translated from dollars into shillings seem enormous.

And there is no perceptible fall in wages going on. On the whole wages tend to rise. For almost all sorts of men, for working women who are not "refined," there is a limitless field of employment. The fact that a growing proportion of the wealth of the community is passing into the hands of a small minority of successful getters, is masked to superficial observation by the enormous increase of the total wealth. The growth process overrides the economic process and may continue to do so for many years.

So that the great mass of the population is not consciously defeated in the economic game. It is only failing to get a large share in the increment of wealth. The European reader must dismiss from his mind any conception of the general American population as a mass of people undergoing impoverishment through the enrichment of the few. He must substitute for that figure a mass of people. very busy, roughly prosperous, generally self-satisfied, but ever and again stirred to bouts of irascibility and suspicion, inundated by a constantly swelling flood of prosperity that pours through it and over it and passes by it, without changing or enriching it at all. Ever and again it is irritated by some rise in price, an advance in coal, for example, or meat or rent, that swallows up some anticipated gain, but that is an entirely different thing from want or distress, from the fireless hungering poverty of Europe.

Nevertheless, the sense of losing develops and spreads in the mass of the American people. Privations are not needed to create a sense of economic disadvantage; thwarted hopes suffice. The speed and pressure of work here is much greater than in

NEW YORK'S CROWDED, LITTERED EAST SIDE

Europe, the impatience for realization intenser. The average American comes into life prepared to "get on," and ready to subordinate most things in life to that. He encounters a rising standard of living. He finds it more difficult to get on than his father did before him. He is perplexed and irritated by the spectacle of lavish spending and the report of gigantic accumulations that outshine his utmost possibilities of enjoyment or success. He is a busy and industrious man, greatly preoccupied by the struggle, but when he stops to think and talk at all, there can be little doubt that his outlook is a disillusioned one, more and more tinged with a deepening discontent.

II

But the state of mind of the average
The Little
Messenger-boy American we have to consider later. That is the central problem of this horoscope we contemplate. Before we come to that we have to sketch out all the broad aspects of the situation with which that mind has to deal.

Now in the preceding chapter I tried to convey my impression of the spending and wealth-getting of this vast community; I tried to convey how irresponsible it was, how unpremeditated. The American rich have, as it were, floated up out of a confused struggle of equal individuals. That indi-

vidualistic commercial struggle has not only flung
up these rich to their own and the world's amaze-
ment, it is also, with an equal blindness, crushing
and maiming great multitudes of souls. But this is
a fact that does not smite upon one's attention
at the outset. The English visitor to the great
towns sees the spending, sees the general prosperity,
the universal air of confident pride; he must go out
of his way to find the under side to these things.

One little thing set me questioning. I had been
one Sunday night down-town, supping and talking
with Mr. Abraham Cahan about the "East Side," that
strange city within a city which has a drama of its
own and a literature and a press, and about Russia
and her problem, and I was returning on the subway about two o'clock in the morning. I became
aware of a little lad sitting opposite me, a childish-
faced delicate little creature of eleven years old or
so, wearing the uniform of a messenger-boy. He
drooped with fatigue, roused himself with a start,
edged off his seat with a sigh, stepped off the car,
and was vanishing up-stairs into the electric glare
of Astor Place as the train ran out of the station.

"What on earth," said I, "is that baby doing
abroad at this time of night?"

For me this weary little wretch became the irri-
tant centre of a painful region of inquiry. "How
many hours a day may a child work in New York,"
I began to ask people, "and when may a boy
leave school?"

CERTAIN WORKERS

I had blundered, I found, upon the weakest spot in America's fine front of national well-being. My eyes were opened to the childish newsboys who sold me papers, and the little bootblacks at the street corners. Nocturnal child employment is a social abomination. I gathered stories of juvenile vice, of lads of nine and ten suffering from terrible diseases, of the contingent sent by these messengers to the hospitals and jails. I began to realize another aspect of that great theory of the liberty of property and the subordination of the state to business, upon which American institutions are based. That theory has no regard for children. Indeed, it is a theory that disregards women and children, the cardinal facts of life altogether. They are private things. . . .

It is curious how little we, who live in the dawning light of a new time, question the intellectual assumptions of the social order about us. We find ourselves in a life of huge confusions and many cruelties, we plan this and that to remedy and improve, but very few of us go down to the ideas that begot these ugly conditions, the laws, the usages and liberties that are now in their detailed expansion so perplexing, intricate, and overwhelming. Yet the life of man is altogether made up of will cast into the mould of ideas, and only by correcting ideas, changing ideas and replacing ideas are any ameliorations and advances to be achieved in human destiny. All other things are subordinate to that.

Now the theory of liberty upon which the liberalism of Great Britain, the Constitution of the United States, and the bourgeois Republic of France rests, assumes that all men are free and equal. They are all tacitly supposed to be adult and immortal, they are sovereign over their property and over their wives and children, and everything is framed with a view to insuring them security in the enjoyment of their rights. No doubt this was a better theory than that of the divine right of kings, against which it did triumphant battle, but it does, as one sees it to-day, fall most extraordinarily short of the truth, and only a few logical fanatics have ever tried to carry it out to its complete consequences. For example, it ignored the facts that more than half of the adult people in a country are women, and that all the men and women of a country taken together are hardly as numerous and far less important to the welfare of that country than the individuals under age. It regarded living as just living, a stupid dead level of egotistical effort and enjoyment; it was blind to the fact that living is part growing, part learning, part dying to make way and altogether service and sacrifice. It asserted that the care and education of children, and business bargains affecting the employment and welfare of women and children, are private affairs. It resisted the compulsory education of children and factory legislation, therefore, with extraordinary persistence and bitterness. The common-

sense of the three great progressive nations concerned has been stronger than their theory, but to
this day enormous social evils are to be traced to
that passionate jealousy of state intervention between a man and his wife, his children, and other
property, which is the distinctive unprecedented
feature of the originally middle-class modern organization of society upon commercial and industrial conceptions in which we are all (and
America most deeply) living.

I began with a drowsy little messenger-boy in the
New York Subway. Before I had done with the
question I had come upon amazing things. Just
think of it! This richest, greatest country the
world has ever seen has over 1,700,000 children under fifteen years of age toiling in fields, factories,
mines, and workshops. And Robert Hunter—whose
Poverty, if I were autocrat, should be compulsory
reading for every prosperous adult in the United
States, tells me of "not less than eighty thousand
children, most of whom are little girls, at present
employed in the textile mills of this country. In
the South there are now six times as many children
at work as there were twenty years ago. Child
labor is increasing yearly in that section of the
country. Each year more little ones are brought
in from the fields and hills to live in the degrading
atmosphere of the mill towns." . . .

Children are deliberately imported by the Italians. I gathered from Commissioner Watchorn at

Ellis Island that the proportion of little nephews and nieces, friends' sons, and so forth, brought in by them is peculiarly high, and I heard him try and condemn a doubtful case. It was a particularly unattractive Italian in charge of a dull-eyed little boy of no ascertainable relationship. . . .

In the worst days of cotton-milling in England the conditions were hardly worse than those now existing in the South. Children, the tiniest and frailest, of five and six years of age, rise in the morning and, like old men and women, go to the mills to do their day's labor; and when they return home, "wearily fling themselves on their beds, too tired to take off their clothes." Many children work all night—"in the maddening racket of the machinery, in an atmosphere unsanitary and clouded with humidity and lint."

"It will be long," adds Mr. Hunter, in his description, "before I forget the face of a little boy of six years, with his hands stretched forward to rearrange a bit of machinery, his pallid face and spare form already showing the physical effects of labor. This child, six years of age, was working twelve hours a day."

From Mr. Spargo's *Bitter Cry of the Children* I learn this much of the joys of certain among the youth of Pennsylvania:

"For ten or eleven hours a day children of ten and eleven stoop over the chute and pick out the slate and other impurities from the coal as it moves past them.

BREAKER BOYS AT A PENNSYLVANIA COLLIERY

The air is black with coal-dust, and the roar of the crushers, screens, and rushing mill-race of coal is deafening. Sometimes one of the children falls into the machinery and is terribly mangled, or slips into the chute and is smothered to death. Many children are killed in this way. Many others, after a time, contract coal - miners' asthma and consumption, which gradually undermine their health. Breathing continually day after day the clouds of coal-dust, their lungs become black and choked with small particles of anthracite." . . .

In Massachusetts, at Fall River, the Hon. J. F. Carey tells us how little naked boys, free Americans, work for Mr. Borden, the New York millionaire, packing cloth into bleaching vats in a bath of chemicals that bleaches their little bodies like the bodies of lepers. . . .

Well, we English have no right to condemn the Americans for these things. The history of our own industrial development is black with the blood of tortured and murdered children. America still has the factory serfs. New Jersey sends her pauper children south to - day into worse than slavery, but, as Cottle tells in his reminiscences of Southey and Coleridge, that is precisely the same wretched export Bristol packed off to feed the mills of Manchester in late Georgian times. We got ahead with factory legislation by no peculiar virtue in our statecraft, it was just the revenge the landlords took upon the manufacturers for reform and free trade in corn and food. In America the manufacturers have had things to themselves.

And America has difficulties to encounter of which we know nothing. In the matter of labor legislation each State legislature is supreme; in each separate State the forces of light and progress must fight the battle of the children and the future over again against interests, lies, prejudice and stupidity. Each State pleads the bad example of another State, and there is always the threat that capital will withdraw. No national minimum is possible under existing conditions. And when the laws have passed there is still the universal contempt for State control to reckon with, the impossibilities of enforcement. Illinois, for instance, scandalized at the spectacle of children in those filthy stock-yards, ankle-deep in blood, cleaning intestines and trimming meat, recently passed a child-labor law that raised the minimum age for such employment to sixteen, but evasion, they told me in Chicago, was simple and easy. New York, too, can show by its statute-books that my drowsy nocturnal messenger - boy was illegal and impossible. . . .

This is the bottomest end of the scale that at the top has all the lavish spending of Fifth Avenue, the joyous wanton giving of Mr. Andrew Carnegie. Equally with these things it is an unpremeditated consequence of an inadequate theory of freedom. The foolish extravagances of the rich, the architectural pathos of Newport, the dingy, noisy, economic jumble of central and south Chicago, the

CERTAIN WORKERS

Standard Oil offices in Broadway, the darkened streets beneath New York's elevated railroad, the littered ugliness of Niagara's banks, and the lowermost hell of child suffering are all so many accordant aspects and inexorable consequences of the same undisciplined way of living. Let each man push for himself—it comes to these things. . . .

So far as our purpose of casting a horoscope goes we have particularly to note this as affecting the future; these working children cannot be learning to read—though they will presently be having votes —they cannot grow up fit to bear arms, to be in any sense but a vile computing sweater's sense, men. So miserably they will avenge themselves by supplying the stuff for vice, for crime, for yet more criminal and political manipulations. One million seven hundred children, practically uneducated, are toiling over here, and growing up, darkened, marred, and dangerous, into the American future I am seeking to forecast.

CHAPTER VIII

CORRUPTION

I

So, it seems to me, in this new crude
The Problem of the Nation continental commonwealth, there is going on the same economic process, on a grander scale, indeed, than has gone so far in our own island. There is a great concentration of wealth above, and below, deep and growing is the abyss, that sunken multitude on the margin of subsistence which is a characteristic and necessary feature of competitive industrialism, that teeming abyss where children have no chance, where men and women dream neither of leisure nor of self-respect. And between this efflorescence of wealth above and spreading degradation below, comes the great mass of the population, perhaps fifty millions and more of healthy and active men, women and children (I leave out of count altogether the colored people and the special trouble of the South until a later chapter) who are neither irresponsibly free nor hopelessly bound, who are the living determining substance of America.

Collectively they constitute what Mr. Roosevelt calls the "Nation," what an older school of Americans used to write of as the People. The Nation is neither rich nor poor, neither capitalist nor laborer, neither Republican nor Democrat; it is a great diversified multitude including all these things. It is a comprehensive abstraction; it is the ultimate reality. You may seek for it in America and you cannot find it, as one seeks in vain for the forest among the trees. It has no clear voice; the confused and local utterances of a dispersed innumerable press, of thousands of public speakers, of books and preachers, evoke fragmentary responses or drop rejected into oblivion. I have been told by countless people where I shall find the typical American; one says in Maine, one in the Alleghenies, one "farther west," one in Kansas, one in Cleveland. He is indeed nowhere and everywhere. He is an English-speaking person, with extraordinarily English traits still, in spite of much good German and Scandinavian and Irish blood he has assimilated. He has a distrust of lucid theories, and logic, and he talks unwillingly of ideas. He is preoccupied, he is busy with his individual affairs, but he is—I can feel it in the air—thinking.

How widely and practically he is thinking that curious product of the last few years, the ten-cent magazine, will show. In England our sixpenny magazines seem all written for boys and careless people; they are nothing but stories and jests and pictures. The weekly ones achieve an extraordinarily agreeable emptiness. Their American equivalents are full of the studied and remarkably wellwritten discussion of grave public questions. I pick up one magazine and find a masterly exposition of the public aspect of railway rebates, another and a trust is analyzed. Then here are some titles of books that all across this continent are being multitudinously read: Parson's *Heart of the Railway Problem*, Steffens's *Shame of the Cities*, Lawson's *Frenzied Finance*, Miss Tarbell's *Story of Standard Oil*, Abbott's *Industrial Problem*, Spargo's *Bitter Cry of the Children*, Hunter's *Poverty*, and, pioneer of them all, Lloyd's *Wealth Against Commonwealth*. These are titles quoted almost at hap-hazard. Within a remarkably brief space of time the American nation has turned away from all the heady self-satisfaction of the nineteenth century and commenced a process of heart searching quite unparalleled in history. Its egotistical interest in its own past is over and done. While Mr. Upton Sinclair, the youngest, most distinctive of recent American novelists, achieved but a secondary success with his admirably conceived romance of the Civil War, *Manassas*, *The Jungle*, his book about the beef trust and the soul of the immigrant, the most unflattering picture of America that any one has yet dared to draw, has fired the country.

The American nation, which a few years ago seemed invincibly wedded to an extreme individualism, seemed resolved, as it were, to sit on the safety valves of the economic process and go on to the ultimate catastrophe, displays itself now alert and questioning. It has roused itself to a grave and extensive consideration of the intricate economic and political problems that close like a net about its future. The essential question for America, as for Europe, is the rescue of her land, her public service, and the whole of her great economic process from the anarchic and irresponsible control of private owners—how dangerous and horrible that control may become the Railway and Beef Trust investigations have shown—and the organization of her social life upon the broad, clean, humane conceptions of modern science. In every country, however, this huge problem of reconstruction which is the alternative to a plutocratic decadence, is enormously complicated by irrelevant and special difficulties. In Great Britain, for example, the ever-pressing problem of holding the empire, and the fact that one legislative body is composed almost entirely of private land-owners, hampers every step towards a better order. Upon every country in Europe weighs the armor of war. In America the complications are distinctive and peculiar. She is free, indeed, now to a large extent from the possibility of any grave military stresses, her one overseas investment in the Philippines she is evidently resolved to forget and be rid of at as early a date as possible. But, on the other hand, she is confronted by a system of legal entanglements of extraordinary difficulty and perplexity, she has the most powerful tradition of individualism in the world, and a degraded political system, and she has in the presence of a vast and increasing proportion of unassimilable aliens in her substance—negroes, south European peasants, Russian Jews and the like—an ever-intensifying complication.

II

Graft

Now what is called corruption in America is a thing not confined to politics; it is a defect of moral method found in every department of American life. I find in big print in every paper I open, "GRAFT." All through my journey in America I have been trying to gauge the quality of this corruption, I have been talking to all kinds of people about it, I have had long conversations about it with President Eliot of Harvard, with District-Attorney Jerome, with one leading insurance president, with a number of the City Club people in Chicago, with several East-Siders in New York, with men engaged in public work in every city I have visited, with Senators at Washington, with a Chicago saloon-keeper and his friend, a shepherd of votes, and with a varied and casual assortment of Americans upon trains and boats; I read my Ostrogorsky, my Otünsterberg, and my Roosevelt before I came to America, and I find myself going through any American newspaper that comes to hand always with an eye to this. It is to me a most vital issue in the horoscope I contemplate. All depends upon the answer to this question: Is the average citizen fundamentally dishonest? Is he a rascal and humbug in grain? If he is, the future can needs be no more than a monstrous social disorganization in the face of divine opportunities. Or is he fundamentally honest, but a little confused ethically? . . .

The latter, I think, is the truer alternative, but I will confess I have ranged through all the scale between a buoyant optimism and despair. It is extraordinarily difficult to move among the crowded contrasts of this perplexing country and emerge with any satisfactory generalization. But there is one word I find all too frequently in the American papers, and that is "stealing." They come near calling any profitable, rather unfair bargain with the public a "steal." It's the common journalistic vice here always to overstate. Every land has its criminals, no doubt, but the American, I am convinced, is the last man in the world to steal. Nor does he tell you lies to your face, except in the way of business. He's not that sort of man. Nor does he sneak bad money into your confiding hand. Nor ask a higher price than he means to accept. Nor cheat on exchange. For all the frequency of "graft" and "stealing" in the press head-lines, I feel the American is pretty distinctly less "mean" than many Europeans in these respects, and much more disposed to be ashamed of meanness.

But he certainly has an ethical system of a highly commercial type. If he isn't dishonest he's commercialized. He lives to get, to come out of every transaction with more than he gave.

In the highly imaginative theory that underlies the realities of an individualistic society there is such a thing as honest trading. In practice I don't believe there is. Exchangeable things are supposed to have a fixed quality called their value, and honest trading is, I am told, the exchange of things of equal value. Nobody gains or loses by honest trading, and therefore nobody can grow rich by it. And nobody would do business except to subsist by a profit and attempt to grow rich. The honest merchant in the individualist's dream is a worthy and urbane person who intervenes between the seller here and the buyer there, fetches from one to another, stores a surplus of goods, takes risks, and indemnifies himself by charging the seller and the buyer a small fee for his waiting and his carrying and his speculative hawking about. He would be sick and ashamed to undervalue a purchase or overcharge a customer, and it scarcely requires a competitor to reduce his fee to a minimum. He draws a line between customers with whom he deals and competitors with whom he wouldn't dream of dealing. And though it seems a little incredible, he grows rich and beautiful in these practices and endows Art, Science, and Literature. Such is the commercial life in a world of economic angels, magic justice and the Individualist's Utopia. In reality flesh and blood cannot resist a bargain, and people trade to get. In reality value is a dream, and the commercial ideal is to buy from the needy, sell to the urgent need, and get all that can possibly be got out of every transaction. To do anything else isn't business — it's some other sort of game. Let us look squarely into the pretences of trading. The plain fact of the case is that in trading for profit there is no natural line at which legitimate bargaining ends and cheating begins. The seller wants to get above the value and the buyer below it. The seller seeks to appreciate, the buyer to depreciate; and where is there room for truth in that contest? In bargaining, overvaluing and undervaluing are not only permissible but inevitable, attempts to increase the desire to buy and willingness to sell. Who can invent a rule to determine what expedients are permissible and what not? You may draw an arbitrary boundary—the law does here and there, a little discontinuously — but that is all. For example, consider these questions that follow: Nothing is perfect in this world; all goods are defective. Are you bound to inform your customer of every defect? Suppose you are, then are you bound to

examine your goods minutely for defects? Grant
that. Then if you intrust that duty to an em-
ployee ought you to dismiss him for selling defective
goods for you? The customer will buy your goods
anyhow. Are you bound to spend more upon cleaning and packing them than he demands?—to wrap
them in gold-foil gratuitously, for example? How
are you going to answer these questions? Let me
suppose that your one dream in life is to grow rich.
Suppose you want to grow very rich and found a
noble university, let us say?

You answer them in the Roman spirit, with
caveat emptor. Then can you decently join in the
outcry against the Chicago butchers?

Then turn again to the group of problems the
Standard Oil history raises. You want the customer to buy your goods and not your competitor's.
Naturally you do everything to get your goods to
him, to make them seem best to him, to reduce the
influx of the other man's stuff. You don't lend
your competitor your shop - window anyhow. If
there's a hoarding you don't restrict your advertisements because otherwise there won't be room
for him. And if you happen to have a paramount
interest in the carrying line that bears your goods
and his, why shouldn't you see that your own goods
arrive first? And at a cheaper rate? . . .

You see one has to admit there is always this
element of overreaching, of outwitting, of fore-
stalling, in all systematic trade. It may be refined,

INTERIOR OF A NEW YORK OFFICE BUILDING

it may be dignified, but it is there. It differs in degree and not in quality from cheating. A very scrupulous man stops at one point, a less scrupulous man at another, an eager, ambitious man may find himself carried by his own impetus very far. Too often the least scrupulous wins. In all ages, among all races, this taint in trade has been felt. Modern western Europe, led by England, and America have denied it stoutly, have glorified the trader, called him a "merchant prince," wrapped him in the purple of the word "financier," bowed down before him. The trader remains a trader, a hand that clutches, an uncreative brain that lays snares. Occasionally, no doubt, he exceeds his function and is better than his occupations. But it is not he but the maker who must be the power and ruler of the great and luminous social order that must surely come, that new order I have persuaded myself I find in glimmering evasive promises amid the congestions of New York, the sheds and defilements of Niagara, and the Chicago reek and grime. . . . The American, I feel assured, can be a bold and splendid maker. He is not, like the, uncreative Parsee or Jew or Armenian, a trader by blood and nature. The architecture I have seen, the finely planned, internally beautiful, and admirably organized office buildings (to step into them from the street is to step up fifty years in the scale of civilization), the business organizations, the industrial skill—I visited a trap and chain factory at Oneida, right in the heart of New York State, that was like the interior of a well-made clock— above all, the plans for reconstructing his cities show that. Those others make nothing. But nevertheless, since he, more than any man, has sub- served the full development of eighteenth and nineteenth century conceptions, he has acquired some of the very worst habits of the trader. Too often he is a gambler. Ever and again I have had glimpses of preoccupied groups of men at green tables in little rooms, playing that dreary game poker, wherein there is no skill, no variety except in the sum at hazard, no orderly development, only a sort of expressionless lying called "bluffing." In- deed, poker isn't so much a game as a bad habit. Yet the American sits for long hours at it, dispers- ing and accumulating dollars, and he carries its great conception of "bluff" and a certain experi- ence of kinetic physiognomy back with him to his office. . . .

And Americans talk dollars to an astonishing extent. . . .

Now this is the reality of American corruption, a huge exclusive preoccupation with dollar - getting. What is called corruption by the press is really no more than the acute expression in individual cases of this general fault.

Where everybody is getting it is idle to expect a romantic standard of honesty between employers and employed. The official who buys rails for the

big railway company that is professedly squeezing
every penny it can out of the public for its shareholders as its highest aim, is not likely to display
any religious self-abnegation of a share for himself
in this great work. The director finds it hard to
distinguish between getting for himself and getting
for his company, and the duty to one-self of a dis-
creet use of opportunity taints the whole staff
from manager to messenger-boy. The politicians
who protect the interests of the same railway in
the House of Commons or the Senate, as the case
may be, are not going to do it for love either. Nobody will have any mercy for their wives or children
if they die poor. The policeman who stands between the property of the company and the irregular enterprise of robbers feels his vigilance merits a
special recognition. A position of trust is a position of advantage, and deserves a percentage.
Everywhere, as every one knows, in all the modern
States, quite as much as in China, there are com-
missions, there are tips, there are extortions and
secret profits, there is, in a word, "graft." It's no
American specialty. Things are very much the
same in this matter in Great Britain as in America,
but Americans talk more and louder than we do.
And indeed all this is no more than an inevitable
development of the idea of trading in the mind,
that every transaction must leave something behind for the agent. It's not stealing, but nevertheless, the automatic cash-register becomes more

and more of a necessity in this thickening atmosphere of private enterprise.

III

IT seems to me that the political
Political Dishonesty corruption that still plays so large a part in the American problem is a natural and necessary underside to a purely middle-class organization of society for business. Nobody is left over to watch the politician. And the evil is enormously aggravated by the complexities of the political machinery, by the methods of the presidential election that practically prescribes a ticket method of voting, and by the absence of any second ballots. Moreover, the passion of the simpler minded Americans for aggressive legislation controlling private morality has made the control of the police a main source of party revenue, and dragged the saloon and brothel, essentially retiring though these institutions are, into politics. The Constitution ties up political reform in the most extraordinary way, it was planned by devout Republicans equally afraid of a dictatorship and the people; it does not so much distribute power as disperse it, the machinery falls readily into the hands of professional politicians with no end to secure but their immediate profit, and is almost inaccessible to poor men who cannot make their

incomes in its working. An increasing number of wealthy young men have followed President Roosevelt into political life—one thinks of such figures as Senator Colby of New Jersey, but they are but incidental mitigations of a generally vicious scheme. Before the nation, so busy with its diversified private affairs, lies the devious and difficult problem of a great reconstruction of its political methods, as a preliminary to any broad change of its social organization. . . .

How vicious things are I have had some inkling in a dozen whispered stories of votes, of ballot-boxes rifled, of votes destroyed, of the violent personation of cowed and ill-treated men. And in Chicago I saw a little of the physical aspect of the system.

I made the acquaintance of Alderman Kenna, who is better known, I found, throughout the States as "Hinky-Dink," saw his two saloons and something of the Chinese quarter about him. He is a compact, upright little man, with iron-gray hair, a clear blue eye, and a dry manner. He wore a bowler hat through all our experiences in common, and kept his hands in his jacket-pockets. He filled me with a ridiculous idea, for which I apologize, that had it fallen to the lot of Mr. J. M. Barrie to miss a university education, and keep a saloon in Chicago and organize voters, he would have looked own brother to Mr. Kenna. We commenced in the first saloon, a fine, handsome place, with mirrors and tables and decorations and a con-

sumption of mitigated mineral waters and beer in
bottles; then I was taken over to see the other
saloon, the one across the way. We went behind
the counter, and while I professed a comparative
interest in English and American beer-engines, and
the Alderman exchanged commonplaces with two
or three of the shirt-sleeved barmen, I was able to
survey the assembled customers.

It struck me as a pretty tough gathering.

The first thing that met the eye were the schooners
of beer. There is nothing quite like the American
beer-schooner in England. It would appeal strongly
to an unstinted appetite for beer, and I should be
curious to try it upon a British agricultural laborer
and see how many he could hold. He would, I am
convinced, have to be entirely hollowed out to hold
two. Those I saw impressed me as being about
the size of small fish-globes set upon stems, and
each was filled with a very substantial-looking beer
indeed. They stood in a careless row all along the
length of the saloon counter. Below them, in attitudes of negligent proprietorship, lounged the
"crowd" in a haze of smoke and conversation.
For the most part I should think they were Americanized immigrants. I looked across the counter
at them, met their eyes, got the quality of their
faces—and it seemed to me I was a very flimsy and
unsubstantial intellectual thing indeed. It struck
me that I would as soon go to live in a pen in a
stock-yard as into American politics.

That was my momentary impression. But that line of base and coarse faces seen through the reek was only one sample of the great saloon stratum of the American population in which resides political power. They have no ideas and they have votes; they are capable, if need be, of meeting violence by violence, and that is the sort of thing American methods demand. . . .

Now Alderman Kenna is a straight man, the sort of man one likes and trusts at sight, and he did not invent his profession. He follows his own ideas of right and wrong, and compared with my ideas of right and wrong, they seem tough, compact, decided things. He is very kind to all his crowd. He helps them when they are in trouble, even if it is trouble with the police; he helps them find employment when they are down on their luck; he stands between them and the impacts of an unsympathetic and altogether too-careless social structure in a sturdy and almost parental way. I can quite believe what I was told, that in the lives of many of these rough undesirables he's almost the only decent influence. He gets wives well treated, and he has an open heart for children. And he tells them how to vote, a duty of citizenship they might otherwise neglect, and sees that they do it properly. And whenever you want to do things in Chicago you must reckon carefully with him. . . .

There you have a chip, a hand specimen, from

the basement structure upon which American politics rest. That is the remarkable alternative to
private enterprise as things are at present. It is
America's only other way. If public services are
to be taken out of the hands of such associations of
financiers as the Standard Oil group they have to
be put into the hands of politicians resting at last
upon this sort of basis. Therein resides the im-
possibility of socialism in America—as the case for
socialism is put at present. The third course is the
far more complex, difficult and heroic one of creating imaginatively and bringing into being a new
state—a feat no people in the world has yet achieved,
but a feat that any people which aspires to lead the
future is bound, I think, to attempt.

CHAPTER IX

THE IMMIGRANT

I

My picture of America assumes now a
<abbr>The Flood</abbr> certain definite form. I have tried to
convey the effect of a great and ener-
getic English - speaking population strewn across a
continent so vast as to make it seem small and thin;
I have tried to show this population caught by the
upward sweep of that great increase in knowledge
that is everywhere enlarging the power and scope of
human effort, exhilarated by it, and active and hopeful beyond any population the world has ever seen,
and I have tried to show how the members of this population struggle and differentiate among themselves
in a universal commercial competition that must, in
the end, if it is not modified, divide them into two
permanent classes of rich and poor. I have vent-
ured to hint at a certain emptiness in the resulting
wealthy, and to note some of the uglinesses and
miseries inseparable from this competition. I have
tried to give my impressions of the vague, yet widely
diffused, will in the nation to resist this differentia-

tion, and of a dim, large movement of thought towards a change of national method. I have glanced at the debasement of politics that bars any immediate hope of such reconstruction. And now it is time to introduce a new element of obstruction and difficulty into this complicating problem—the immigrants.

Into the lower levels of the American community there pours perpetually a vast torrent of strangers, speaking alien tongues, inspired by alien traditions, for the most part illiterate peasants and working-people. They come in at the bottom: that must be insisted upon. An enormous and ever-increasing proportion of the laboring classes, of all the lower class in America, is of recent European origin, is either of foreign birth or foreign parentage. The older American population is being floated up on the top of this influx, a sterile aristocracy above a racially different and astonishingly fecund proletariat. (For it grows rankly in this new soil. One section of immigrants, the Hungarians, have here a birth-rate of forty-six in the thousand, the highest of any civilized people in the world.)

Few people grasp the true dimensions of this invasion. Figures carry so little. The influx has clambered from half a million to 700,000, to 800,000; this year the swelling figures roll up as if they mean to go far over the million mark. The flood swells to overtake the total birth-rate; it has already over-topped the total of births of children to native-American parents.

THE IMMIGRANT

I have already told something of the effect of Ellis Island. I have told how I watched the long procession of simple - looking, hopeful, sunburned country folk from Russia, from the Carpathians, from southern Italy and Turkey and Syria, filing through the wickets, bringing their young wives for the mills of Paterson and Fall River, their children for the Pennsylvania coal-breakers and the cotton-mills of the South.

Yet there are moments when I could have imagined there were no immigrants at all. All the time, except for one distinctive evening, I seem to have been talking to English-speaking men, now and then to the Irishman, now and then, but less frequently, to an Americanized German. In the clubs there are no immigrants. There are not even Jews, as there are in London clubs. One goes about the wide streets of Boston, one meets all sorts of Boston people, one visits the State-House; it's all the authentic English-speaking America. Fifth Avenue, too, is America without a touch of foreign-born; and Washington. You go a hundred yards south of the pretty Boston Common and, behold! you are in a polyglot slum! You go a block or so east of Fifth Avenue and you are in a vaster, more Yiddish White-chapel. You cross from New York to Staten Island, attracted by its distant picturesque suggestion of scattered homes among the trees, and you discover black-tressed, bold-eyed women on those pleasant verandas, half-clad brats, and ambiguous washing, where once the native American held his simple state. You ask the way of a young man who has just emerged from a ramshackle factory, and you are answered in some totally incomprehensible tongue. You come up again after such a dive below, to dine with the original Americans again, talk with them, go about with them and forget. . . .

In Boston, one Sunday afternoon, this fact of immigration struck upon Mr. Henry James:

"There went forward across the cop of the hill a continuous passage of men and women, in couples and talkative companies, who struck me as laboring wage-earners of the simpler sort arrayed in their Sunday best and decently enjoying their leisure . . . no sound of English in a single instance escaped their lips; the greater number spoke a rude form of Italian, the others some outland dialect unknown to me— though I waited and waited to catch an echo of antique refrains."

That's one of a series of recurrent, uneasy observations of this great replacement I find in Mr. James's book.

The immigrant does not clamor for attention. He is, indeed, almost entirely inaudible, inarticulate, and underneath. He is in origin a peasant, inarticulate, and underneath by habit and tradition. Mr. James has, as it were, to put his ear to earth, to catch the murmuring of strange tongues. The incomer is of diverse nationality and diverse tongues, and that "breaks him up" politically and socially. He drops into American clothes, and then he does not catch the careless eye. He goes into special regions and works there. Where Americans talk or think or have leisure to observe, he does not intrude. The bulk of the Americans don't get as yet any real sense of his portentous multitude at all. He does not read very much, and so he produces no effect upon the book trade or magazines. You can go through such a periodical as *Harper's Magazine*, for example, from cover to cover, and unless there is some article or story bearing specifically upon the subject you might doubt if there was an immigrant in the country. On the liner coming over, at Ellis Island, and sometimes on the railroads one saw him—him and his womankind,—in some picturesque east-European garb, very respectful, very polite, adventurous, and a little scared. Then he became less visible. He had got into cheap American clothes, resorted to what naturalists call "protective mimicry," even perhaps acquired a collar. Also his bearing had changed, become charged with a certain aggression. He had got a pocket-handkerchief, and had learned to move fast and work fast, and to chew and spit with the proper meditative expression. One detected him by his diminishing accent, and by a few persistent traits—rings in his ears, perhaps, or the like adornment. In the next stage these also had gone; he had become ashamed of the music of his native tongue, and talked even to his wife, on the trolley-car and other public places, at least, in brief remarkable American. Before that he had become ripe for a vote.

The next stage of Americanization, I suppose, is this dingy quick-eyed citizen with his schooner of beer in my Chicago saloon—if it is not that crumpled thing I saw lying so still in the sunlight under the trestle bridge on my way to Washington. . . .

II

EVERY American above forty, and In Defence of most of those below that limit, seem Immigration to be enthusiastic advocates of unrestricted immigration. I could not make them understand the apprehension with which this huge dilution of the American people with profoundly ignorant foreign peasants filled me. I rode out on an automobile into the pretty New York country beyond Yonkers with that finely typical American, Mr. Z.—he wanted to show me the pleasantness of the land,—and he sang the song of American confidence, I think, more clearly and loudly than any. He told me how everybody had hope, how everybody had incentive, how magnificently it was all going on. He told me—what is, I am afraid, a widely spread delusion—that elementary education stands on a higher level of efficiency in the States than in England. He had no doubt whatever of

138

the national powers of assimilation. "Let them all come," he said, cheerfully.

"The Chinese?" said I.

"We can do with them all." . . .

He was exceptional in that extension. Most Americans stop at the Ural Mountains, and refuse the "Asiatic." It was not a matter for discussion with him, but a question of belief. He had ceased to reason about immigration long ago. He was a man in the fine autumn of life, abounding in honors, wrapped in furs, and we drove swiftly in his automobile, through the spring sunshine. ("By Jove!" thought I, "you talk like Pippa's rich uncle.") By some half-brother of a coincidence we happened first upon this monument commemorating a memorable incident of the War of Independence, and then upon that. He recalled details of that great campaign as Washington was fought out of Manhattan northward. I remember one stone among the shooting trees that indicated where in the Hudson River near by a British sloop had fired the first salute in honor of the American flag. That salute was vividly present still to him; it echoed among the woods, it filled him with a sense of personal triumph; it seemed halfway back to Agincourt to me. All that bright morning the stars and stripes made an almost luminous visible presence about us. Open-handed hospitality and confidence in God so swayed me that it is indeed only now, as I put this book together, I see this shining buoyancy, this bunting patriotism, in its direct relation to the Italian babies in the cotton-mills, to the sinister crowd that stands in the saloon smoking and drinking beer, an accumulating reserve of unintelligent force behind the manœuvres of the professional politicians. . . .

I tried my views upon Commissioner Watchorn as we leaned together over the gallery railing and surveyed that bundle-carrying crowd creeping step by step through the wire filter of the central hall of Ellis Island—into America.

"You don't think they'll swamp you?" I said.

"Now look here," said the Commissioner, "I'm English born—Derbyshire. I came into America when I was a lad. I had fifteen dollars. And here I am! Well, do you expect me, now I'm here, to shut the door on any other poor chaps who want a start — a start with hope in it, in the New World?"

A pleasant-mannered, a fair-haired young man, speaking excellent English, had joined us as we went round, and nodded approval.

I asked him for his opinion, and gathered he was from Milwaukee, and the son of a Scandinavian immigrant. He, too, was for "fair-play" and an open door for every one. "Except," he added, "Asiatics." So also, I remember, was a very New England lady I met at Hull House, who wasn't, as a matter of fact, a New-Englander at all, but the daughter of a German settler in the Middle West. They all seemed to think that I was inspired by hostility to the im-

migrant in breathing any doubt about the desir-
ability of this immense process. . . .

I tried in each case to point out that this idea of
not being churlishly exclusive did not exhaust the
subject, that the present immigration is a different
thing entirely from the immigration of half a century
ago, that in the interest of the immigrant and his
offspring more than any one, is the protest to be
made. Fifty years ago more than half of the torrent was English speaking, and the rest mostly from
the Teutonic and Scandinavian northwest of Europe,
an influx of people closely akin to the native Americans in temperament and social tradition. They
were able to hold their own and mix perfectly. Even
then the quantity of illiterate Irish produced a
marked degradation of political life. The earlier
immigration was an influx of energetic people who
wanted to come, and who had to put themselves to
considerable exertion to get here; it was higher in
character and in social quality than the present flood.
The immigration of to-day is largely the result of
energetic canvassing by the steamship companies;
it is, in the main, an importation of laborers and not
of economically independent settlers, and it is increasingly alien to the native tradition. The bulk
of it is now Italian, Russian Jewish, Russian, Hun-
garian, Croatian, Roumanian, and eastern European
generally.

"The children learn English, and become more
American and better patriots than the Americans,"

Commissioner Watchorn—echoing everybody in that
—told me. . . .

(In Boston one optimistic lady looked to the
Calabrian and Sicilian peasants to introduce an
artistic element into the population—no doubt because they come from the same peninsula that produced the Florentines.)

III

WILL the reader please remember that
Assimilation I've been just a few weeks in the States
altogether, and value my impressions
at that! And will he, nevertheless, read of doubts
that won't diminish. I doubt very much if America
is going to assimilate all that she is taking in now;
much more do I doubt that she will assimilate the
still greater inflow of the coming years. I believe
she is going to find infinite difficulties in that task.
By "assimilate" I mean make intelligently co-opera-
tive citizens of these people. She will, I have no
doubt whatever, impose upon them a bare use of the
English language, and give them votes and certain
patriotic persuasions, but I believe that if things
go on as they are going the great mass of them will
remain a very low lower class—will remain largely
illiterate industrialized peasants. They are decent-
minded peasant people, orderly, industrious people,
rather dirty in their habits, and with a low standard

of life. Wherever they accumulate in numbers they present to my eye a social phase far below the level of either England, France, north Italy, or Switzerland. And, frankly, I do not find the American nation has either in its schools—which are as backward in some States as they are forward in others— in its press, in its religious bodies or its general tone, any organized means or effectual influences for raising these huge masses of humanity to the requirements of an ideal modern civilization. They are, to my mind, "biting off more than they can chaw" in this matter.

I got some very interesting figures from Dr. Hart, of the Children's Home and Aid Society, Chicago, in this matter. He was pleading for the immigrant against my scepticisms. He pointed out to me that the generally received opinion that the European immigrants are exceptionally criminal is quite wrong.

The 1900 census report collapsed after a magnificent beginning, and its figures are not available, but from the earlier records there can be no doubt that the percentage of criminals among the "foreign-born" is higher than that among the native-born. This, however, is entirely due to the high criminal record of the French Canadians in the Northeast, and the Mexicans in Arizona, who are not over-seas immigrants at all. The criminal statistics of the French Canadians in the States should furnish useful matter for the educational controversy in Great Britain. Allowing for their activities—which appear to be

based on an education of peculiar religious virtue—
the figures bring the criminal percentage among the
foreigners far below that of the native-born. But
Dr. Hart's figures also showed very clearly something further: as between the offspring of native and
foreign parents the preponderance of crime is enormously on the side of the latter.

That, at any rate, falls in with my own precon-
ceptions and roving observations. Bear in mind
always that this is just one questioning individual's
impression. It seems to me that the immigrant
arrives an artless, rather uncivilized, pious, good-
hearted peasant, with a disposition towards submissive industry and rude effectual moral habits.
America, it is alleged, makes a man of him. It
seems to me that all too often she makes an in-
furiated toiler of him, tempts him with dollars and
speeds him up with competition, hardens him,
coarsens his manners, and, worst crime of all, lures
and forces him to sell his children into toil. The
home of the immigrant in America looks to me worse
than the home he came from in Italy. It is just as
dirty, it is far less simple and beautiful, the food is
no more wholesome, the moral atmosphere far less
wholesome; and, as a consequence, the child of the
immigrant is a worse man than his father.

I am fully aware of the generosity, the nobility of
sentiment which underlies the American objection to
any hindrance to immigration. But either that
general sentiment should be carried out to a logical

completeness and a gigantic and costly machinery organized to educate and civilize these people as they come in, or it should be chastened to restrict the inflow to numbers assimilable under existing conditions. At present, if we disregard sentiment, if we deny the alleged need of gross flattery whenever one writes of America for Americans, and state the bare facts of the case, they amount to this: that America, in the urgent process of individualistic industrial development, in its feverish haste to get through with its material possibilities, is importing a large portion of the peasantry of central and eastern Europe, and converting it into a practically illiterate industrial proletariat. In doing this it is doing a something that, however different in spirit, differs from the slave trade of its early history only in the narrower gap between employer and laborer. In the "colored" population America has already ten million descendants of unassimilated and perhaps unassimilable labor immigrants. These people are not only half civilized and ignorant, but they have infected the white population about them with a kindred ignorance. For there can be no doubt that if an Englishman or Scotchman of the year 1500 were to return to earth and seek his most retrograde and decivilized descendants, he would find them at last among the white and colored population south of Washington. And I have a foreboding that in this mixed flood of workers that pours into America by the million to-day, in this torrent of ignorance, against which that heroic being, the schoolmarm, battles at present all unaided by men, there is to be found the possibility of another dreadful separation of class and kind, a separation perhaps not so profound but far more universal. One sees the possibility of a rich industrial and mercantile aristocracy of western European origin, dominating a darker-haired, darker-eyed, uneducated proletariat from central and eastern Europe. The immigrants are being given votes, I know, but that does not free them, it only enslaves the country. The negroes were given votes.

That is the quality of the danger as I see it. But before this indigestion of immigrants becomes an incurable sickness of the States many things may happen. There is every sign, as I have said, that a great awakening, a great disillusionment, is going on in the American mind. The Americans have become suddenly self-critical, are hot with an unwonted fever for reform and constructive effort. This swamping of the country may yet be checked. They may make a strenuous effort to emancipate children below fifteen from labor, and so destroy one of the chief inducements of immigration. Once convince them that their belief in the superiority of their public schools to those of England and Germany is an illusion, or at least that their schools are inadequate to the task before them, and it may be they will perform some swift American miracle of educational organization and finance. For all the very heavy special educational charges that are needed if the immigrant is really to be assimilated, it seems a reasonable proposal that immigration should pay. Suppose the new-comer were presently to be taxed on arrival for his own training and that of any children he had with him, that again would check the inrush very greatly. Or the steamship company might be taxed, and left to settle the trouble with the immigrant by raising his fare. And finally, it may be that if the line is drawn, as it seems highly probable it will be, at "Asiatics," then there may even be a drying up of the torrent at its source. The European countries are not unlimited reservoirs of offspring. As they pass from their old conditions into more and more completely organized modern industrial states, they develop a new internal equilibrium and cease to secrete an excess of population. England no longer supplies any great quantity of Americans; Scotland barely any; France is exhausted; Ireland, Germany, Scandinavia have, it seems, disgorged nearly all their surplus load, and now run dry. . . .

These are all mitigations of the outlook, but still the dark shadow of disastrous possibility remains. The immigrant comes in to weaken and confuse the counsels of labor, to serve the purposes of corruption, to complicate any economic and social development, above all to retard enormously the development of that national consciousness and will on which the hope of the future depends.

THE FUTURE IN AMERICA

IV

I TOLD these doubts of mine to a pleasant young lady of New York, who seems to find much health and a sustaining happiness in settlement work on the East Side. She scorned my doubts. "Children make better citizens than the old Americans," she said, like one who quotes a classic, and took me with her forthwith to see the central school of the Educational Alliance, that fine imposing building in East Broadway.

It's a thing I'm glad not to have missed. I recall a large cool room with a sloping floor, tier rising above tier of seats and desks, and a big class of bright-eyed Jewish children, boys and girls, each waving two little American flags to the measure of the song they sang, singing to the accompaniment of the piano on the platform beside us.

"God bless our native land," they sang—with a considerable variety of accent and distinctness, but with a very real emotion.

Some of them had been in America a month, some much longer, but here they were—under the auspices of the wealthy Hebrews of New York and Mr. Blaustein's enthusiastic direction—being Americanized. They sang of America — "sweet land of liberty"; they stood up and drilled with the little bright pretty flags; swish they crossed and swish they waved back, a waving froth of flags and flushed

WHERE IMMIGRANT CHILDREN ARE AMERICANIZED

children's faces; and they stood up and repeated the oath of allegiance, and at the end filed tramping by me and out of the hall. The oath they take is finely worded. It runs:

"Flag our great Republic, inspirer in battle, guardian of our homes, whose stars and stripes stand for bravery, purity, truth, and union, we salute thee! We, the natives of distant lands, who find rest under thy folds, do pledge our hearts, our lives, and our sacred honor to love and protect thee, our country, and the liberty of the American people forever."

I may have been fanciful, but as I stood aside and watched them going proudly past, it seemed to me that eyes met mine, triumphant and victorious eyes —for was I not one of these British from whom freedom was won? But that was an ignoble suspicion. They had been but a few weeks in America, and that light in their eyes was just a brotherly challenge to one they supposed a fellow-citizen who stood unduly thoughtful amid their rhythmic exaltation. They tramped out and past with their flags and guidons.

"It *is* touching!" whispered my guide, and I saw she had caught a faint reflection of that glow that lit the children.

I told her it was the most touching thing I had seen in America.

And so it remains.

Think of the immense promise in it! Think of the flower of belief and effort that may spring from this warm sowing! We passed out of this fluttering multiplication of the most beautiful flag in the world, into streets abominable with offal and indescribable filth, and dark and horrible under the thunderous girders of the Elevated railroad, to our other quest for that morning, a typical New York tenement. For I wanted to see one, with practically windowless bedrooms. . . .

The Educational Alliance is of course not a public institution; it was organized by Hebrews, and conducted for Hebrews, chiefly for the benefit of the Hebrew immigrant. It is practically the only organized attempt to Americanize the immigrant child. After the children have mastered sufficient English and acquired the simpler elements of patriotism—which is practically no more than an emotional attitude towards the flag—they pass on into the ordinary public schools.

"Yes," I told my friend, "I know how these children feel. That, less articulate perhaps, but no less sincere, is the thing — something between pride and a passionate desire — that fills three-quarters of the people at Ellis Island now. They come ready to love and worship, ready to bow down and kiss the folds of your flag. They give themselves—they want to give. Do you know I, too, have come near feeling that at times for America." . . .

We were separated for a while by a long hole in the middle of the street and a heap of builder's refuse. Before we came within talking distance again I was in reaction against the gleam of satisfaction my last confession had evoked.

"In the end," I said, "you Americans won't be able to resist it."

"Resist what?"

"You'll respect your country," I said.

"What do you mean?"

In those crowded noisy East Side streets one has to shout, and shout compact things. "*This!*" I said to the barbaric disorder about us. "Lynching! Child Labor! Graft!"

Then we were separated by a heap of decaying fish that some hawker had dumped in the gutter.

My companion shouted something I did not catch.

"*We'll* tackle it!" she repeated.

I looked at her, bright and courageous and youthful, a little overconfident, I thought, but extremely reassuring, going valiantly through a disorderly world of obstacles, and for the moment — I suppose that waving bunting and the children's voices had got into my head a little—I forgot all sorts of things. . . .

I could have imagined her the spirit of America incarnate rather than a philanthropic young lady of New York.

CHAPTER X

STATE-BLINDNESS

I

In what I have written so far, I have Sense of the State tried to get the effect of the American outlook, the American task, the American problem as a whole, as it has presented itself to me. Clearly, as I see it, it is a mental and moral issue. There seems to me an economic process going on that tends to concentrate first wealth and then power in the hands of a small number of adventurous individuals of no very high intellectual type, a huge importation of alien and unassimilable workers, and a sustained disorder of local and political administration. Correlated with this is a great increase in personal luxury and need. In all these respects there is a strong parallelism between the present condition of the United States and the Roman Republic in the time of the early Cæsars; and arguing from these alone one might venture to forecast the steady development of an exploiting and devastating plutocracy, leading perhaps to Cæsarism, and a progressive decline in civilization and social

152

solidarity. But there are forces of recuperation and construction in America such as the earlier instance did not display. There is infinitely more original and originating thought in the state, there are the organized forces of science, a habit of progress, clearer and wider knowledge among the general mass of the people. These promise, and must, indeed, inevitably make, some synthetic effort of greater or less homogeneity and force. It is upon that synthetic effort that the distinctive destiny of America depends.

I propose to go on now to discuss the mental quality of America as I have been able to focus it. (Remember always that I am an undiplomatic tourist of no special knowledge or authority, who came, moreover, to America with certain prepossessions.) And first, and chiefly, I have to convey what seems to me the most significant and pregnant thing of all. It is a matter of something wanting, that the American shares with the great mass of prosperous middle-class people in England. I think it is best indicated by saying that the typical American has no "sense of the state." I do not mean that he is not passionately and vigorously patriotic. But I mean that he has no perception that his business activities, his private employments, are constituents in a large collective process; that they affect other people and the world forever, and cannot, as he imagines, begin and end with him. He sees the world in fragments; it is to him a multitudinous

153

collection of individual "stories" — as the newspapers put it. If one studies an American newspaper,
one discovers it is all individuality, all a matter of
personal doings, of what so and so said and how so
and so felt. And all these individualities are un-
fused. Not a touch of abstraction or generalization,
no thinnest atmosphere of reflection, mitigates these
harsh, emphatic, isolated happenings. The American, it seems to me, has yet to achieve what is,
after all, the product of education and thought,
the conception of a whole to which all individual
acts and happenings are subordinate and contrib-
utory.

When I say this much, I do not mean to insinuate
that any other nation in the world has any superiority
in this matter. But I do want to urge that the
American problem is pre-eminently one that must
be met by broad ways of thinking, by creative,
synthetic, and merging ideas, and that a great number of Americans seem to lack these altogether.

II

A Sample
American
LET me by way of illustration give a
specimen American mind. It is not the
mind of a writer or philosopher, it is
just a plain successful business - man who exposes
himself, and makes it clear that this want of any
sense of the state of any large duty of constructive

loyalty, is not an idiosyncrasy, but the quality of all his circle, his friends, his religious teacher. . . .

I found my specimen in a book called *With John Bull and Jonathan*. It contains the rather rambling reminiscences of Mr. J. Morgan Richards, the wealthy and successful London agent of a great number of well - advertised American proprietary articles, and I read it first, I will confess, chiefly in search of such delightful phrases as the one "mammoth in character" I have already quoted. But there were few to equal that first moment's bright discovery. What I got from it finally wasn't so much that sort of thing as this realization of Mr. Richards's peculiar quality, this acute sense of all that he hadn't got. Mr. Richards told of advertising enterprises, of contracts and journeyings, of his great friendship with the late Dr. Parker, of his domestic affairs, and all the changes in the world that had struck him, and of a remarkable dining club, called (paradoxically) the *Sphinx*, in which the giants (or are they the mammoths?) of the world of advertisement foregather. He gave his portrait, and the end-paper presented him playfully as the jolly president of the Sphinx Club, champagne-bottle crowned, but else an Egyptian monarch; and on the cover are two gilt hands clasped across a gilt ripple of sea ("hands across the sea"), under intertwining English and American flags. From the book one got an effect, garrulous perhaps, but on the whole not unpleasing, of an elderly but still active

155

business personality quite satisfied by his achievements, and representative of I know not what proportion, but at any rate a considerable proportion, of his fellow-countrymen. And one got an effect of a being not simply indifferent to the health and vigor and growth of the community of which he was a part, but unaware of its existence.

He displays this irresponsibility of the commercial mind so illuminatingly because he does in a way attempt to tell something more than his personal story. He notes the changes in the world about him, how this has improved and that progressed, which contrasts between England and America struck upon his mind. That he himself is responsible amid these changes never seems to dawn upon him. His freedom from any sense of duty to the world as a whole, of any subordination of trading to great ideas, is naïve and fundamental. He tells of how he arranged with the authorities in charge of the Independence Day celebrations on Boston Common to display "three large pieces" containing the name of a certain "bitters," which they did, and how this no doubt very desirable commodity was first largely advertised throughout the United States in the fall of 1861, and rapidly became the success of the day, because of the enormous amount of placarding given to the cabalistic characters 'S - T - 1860 - X.' Those strange letters and figures stared upon people from wall and fence and tree, in every leading town throughout the United States. They were painted on the rocks of the Hudson River to such an extent that the attention of the Legislature was drawn to the fact, and a law was passed to prevent the further disfigurement of river scenery."

He calls this "cute." He tells, too, of his educational work upon the English press, how he won it over to "display" advertisements, and devised "the first sixteen-sheet double-demy poster ever seen in England in connection with a proprietary article." He introduced the smoking of cigarettes into England against great opposition. Mr. Richards finds no incongruity, but apparently a very delightful association, in the fact that this great victory for the adolescent's cigarette was won on the site of Strudwick's house, wherein John Bunyan died, and hard by the path of the Smithfield martyrs to their fiery sacrifice. Both they and Mr. Richards "lit such a candle in England—"

Well, my business is not to tell of the feats by which Mr. Richards grew wealthy and important as a tree may grow and flourish amid the masonry it helps to disintegrate. My business is purely with his insensibility to the state as an aspect of his personal life. It is insensibility — not disregard or hostility. One gets an impression from this book that if Mr. Richards had lived in a different culture, he would have been a generous giver of himself. In spite of his curious incapacity to appreciate any issues larger than large enterprises in selling, he is very evidently a religious man. He sat under the late

Dr. Parker of the rich and prosperous City Temple, and that reverend gentleman's leonine visage adorns the book. Its really the light one gets on Dr. Parker and his teaching that appeals to me most in this volume. For this gentleman Mr. Richards seems to have entertained a feeling approaching reverence. He notes such details as:

"At the conclusion of an invocation or prayer, his habit always was to make a pause of a few seconds before pronouncing 'Amen.' This was most impressive. . . .

"He spoke such words as 'God,' 'Jesus Christ,' 'No,' 'Yes,' 'Nothing,' in a way to give more value to each word than any speaker I have ever heard."

They became great friends, rarely a week passed without their meeting, and, says Mr. Richards, he "was pleased, in the course of time, to honor me with his confidence in a marked degree, as though he recognized in me some quality which satisfied his judgment, that I could be trusted in business questions quite apart from those relating to his church. He was not only a born preacher, but possessed a marvellous grasp of sound, practical knowledge upon the affairs of the day. I often consulted with him regarding my own affairs, always getting the most practical help."

When Dr. Parker came to America, the two friends corresponded warmly, and several of the letters are quoted. Even "£5000 a year easily made" could not tempt him from London and the modest opulence of the City Temple. . . .

But my business now is not to dwell on these characteristic details, but to point out that Mr. Richards does not stand alone in the entire detachment, not only of his worldly achievements, but of his spiritual life, from any creative solicitude for the state. If he was merely an isolated "character" I should have no concern with him. His association with Dr. Parker shows most luminously that he presents a whole cult of English and American rich traders, who in America "sat under" such men as the Rev. Henry Ward Beecher, for example, who evidently stand for much more in America than in England, and who, so far as the state and political and social work go, are scarcely of more use, are probably more hindrance, than any organization of selfish voluptuaries of equal wealth and numbers. It is a cult, it has its teachers and its books. I have had a glimpse of one of its manuals. I find Mr. Richards quoting with approval Dr. Parker's "Ten General Commandments for Men of Business," commandments which strike me as not only State-blind, but utterly God-blind, which are, indeed, no more than shrewd counsels for "getting on." It is really quite horrible stuff morally. "Thou shalt not hobnob with idle persons," parodies Dr. Parker in commandment V., so glossing richly upon the teachings of Him who ate with publicans and sinners, and (no doubt to instil the advisability of keeping one's more

delicate business procedure in one's own hands),
"Thou shalt not forget that a servant who can tell
lies *for* thee, may one day tell lies *to* thee." . . .

I am not throwing any doubt upon the sincerity
of Dr. Parker and Mr. Richards. I believe that
nothing could exceed the transparent honesty that
ends this record which tells of a certain bitters
pushed at the sacrifice of beautiful scenery, of a
successful propaganda of cigarette-smoking, and of
all sorts of proprietary articles landed well home in
their gastric target of a whole life lost, indeed, in
commercial self-seeking, with "What shall I render
unto the Lord for all his benefits?"

> " The Now is an atom of Sand,
>   And the Near is a perishing Clod,
>   But Afar is a fairyland,
>   And Beyond is the Bosom of God."

What I have to insist upon now is that this is a
sample, and, so far as I can tell, a fair sample, of the
quality and trend of the mind-stuff and the breadth
and height of the tradition of a large and I know
not how influential mass of prosperous middle-
class English, and of a much more prosperous and influential and important section of Americans. They
represent much energy, they represent much property, they are a factor to reckon with. They present a powerful opposing force to anything that will
suppress their disgusting notice-boards or analyze
their ambiguous "proprietary articles," or tax their

gettings for any decent public purpose. And here I find them selling poisons as pain-killers, and alcohol as tonics, and fighting ably and boldly to silence adverse discussion. In the face of the great needs that lie before America their active trivality of soul, their energy and often unscrupulous activity, and their quantitative importance become, to my mind, adverse and threatening, a stumbling-block for hope. For the impression I have got by going to and fro in America is that Mr, Richards is a fair sample of at least the older type of American. So far as I can learn, Mr. J. D. Rockefeller is just another product of the same cult. You meet these older types everywhere, they range from fervent piety and temperance to a hearty drinking, "story"-telling, poker-playing type, but they have in common a sharp, shrewd, narrow, business habit of mind that ignores the future and the state altogether. But I do not find the younger men are following in their lines. Some are. But just how many and to what extent, I do not know. It is very hard for a literary man to estimate the quantity and importance of ideas in a community. The people he meets naturally all entertain ideas, or they would not come in his way. The people who have new ideas talk; those who have not, go about their business. But I hazard an opinion that Young America now presents an altogether different type from the young men of enterprise and sound Baptist and business principles who were the backbone of the irresponsible commercial

America of yesterday, the America that rebuilt Chicago on "floating foundations," covered the world with advertisement boards, gave the great cities the elevated railroads, and organized the trusts.

III

I SPENT a curious day amid the memories of that strangely interesting social experiment, the Oneida Community, and met a most significant contemporary, "live American" of the newer school, in the son of the founder and the present head of "Oneida Limited."

Oneida

There are moments when that visit I paid to Oneida seems to me to stand for all America. The place, you know, was once the seat of a perfectionist community; the large red community buildings stand now among green lawns and ripening trees, and I dined in the communal dining-room, and visited the library, and saw the chain and trap factory, and the silk-spinning factory and something of all its industries. I talked to old and middle-aged people who told me all sorts of interesting things of "community days," looked through curious old-fashioned albums of photographs, showing the women in their bloomers and cropped hair, and the men in the ill-fitting frock-coats of the respectable mediocre person in early Victorian times. I think that some of the reminiscences I awakened had been voiceless for some time. At moments it was like hearing the story of a flattened, dry, and colorless flower between the pages of a book, of a verse written in faded ink, or of some daguerreotype spotted and faint beyond recognition. It was extraordinarily New England in its quality as I looked back at it all. They claimed a quiet perfection of soul, they searched one another marvellously for spiritual chastening, they defied custom and opinion, they followed their reasoning and their theology to the inmost amazing abnegations—and they kept themselves solvent by the manufacture of steel traps that catch the legs of beasts in their strong and pitiless jaws. . . .

But this book is not about the things that concerned Oneida in community days, and I mention them here only because of the curious developments of the present time. Years ago, when the founder, John Humphrey Noyes, grew old and unable to control the new dissensions that arose out of the sceptical attitude of the younger generation towards his ingenious theology, and such-like stresses, communism was abandoned, the religious life and services discontinued, the concern turned into a joint-stock company, and the members made shareholders on strictly commercial lines. For some years its prosperity declined. Many of the members went away. But a nucleus remained as residents in the old buildings, and after a time there were returns.

I was told that in the early days of the new period there was a violent reaction against communistic methods, a jealous inexperienced insistence upon property. "It was difficult to borrow a hammer," said one of my informants.

Then, as the new generation began to feel its feet, came a fresh development of vitality. The Oneida company began to set up new machinery, to seek wider markets, to advertise and fight competitors.

This Mr. P. B. Noyes was the leader into the new paths. He possesses all the force of character, the constructive passion, the imaginative power of his progenitor, and it has all gone into business competition. I have heard much talk of the romance of business, chiefly from people I heartily despised, but in Mr. Noyes I found business indeed romantic. It had got hold of him, it possessed him like a passion. He has inspired all his half-brothers and cousins and younger fellow-members of the community with his own imaginative motive. They, too, are enthusiasts for business.

Mr. Noyes is a tall man, who looks down when he talks to one. He showed me over the associated factories, told me how the trap trade of all North America is in Oneida's hands, told me of how they fight and win against the British traps in South America and Burmah. He showed me photographs of panthers in traps, tigers in traps, bears snarling at death, unfortunate deer, foxes caught by the paws. . . .

I did my best to forget those photographs at once in the interest of his admirable machinery, which busied itself with chain-making as though it had eyes and hands. I went beside him, full of that respect that a literary man must needs feel when a creative business controller displays his quality.

"But the old religion of Oneida?" I would interpolate.

"Each one of us is free to follow his own religion. Here is a new sort of chain we are making for hanging-lamps. Hitherto—"

Presently I would try again. "Are the workers here in any way members of the community?"

"Oh no! Many of them are Italian immigrants. We think of building a school for them. . . . No, we get no labor troubles. We pay always above the trade-union rates, and so we get the pick of the workmen. Our class of work can't be sweated." . . .

Yes, he was an astonishing personality, so immensely concentrated on these efficient manufacturing and trading developments, so evidently careless of theology, philosophy, social speculation, beauty.

"Your father was a philosopher," I said.

"I think in ten years' time I may give up the control here," he threw out, "and write something."

"I've thought of the publishing trade myself," I said, "when my wits are old and stiff." . . .

I never met a man before so firmly gripped by the romantic constructive and adventurous element of business, so little concerned about personal riches or the accumulation of wealth. He illuminated much that had been dark to me in the American character. I think better of business by reason of him. And time after time I tried him upon politics. It came to nothing. Making a new world was, he thought, a rhetorical flourish about futile and troublesome activities, and politicians merely a disreputable sort of parasite upon honorable people who made chains and plated spoons. All his constructive instincts, all his devotion, were for Oneida and its enterprises. America was just the impartial space, the large liberty, in which Oneida grew, the Stars and Stripes a wide sanction akin to the impartial irresponsible harboring sky overhead. Sense of the State had never grown in him—can now, I felt convinced, never grow. . . .

But some day, I like to imagine, the World State, and not Oneida corporations, and a nobler trade than traps, will command such services as his.

CHAPTER XI

TWO STUDIES IN DISAPPOINTMENT

I

IN considering the quality of the
The Riddle of American mind (upon which, as I be-
Intolerance
lieve, the ultimate destiny of America
entirely depends), it has been necessary to point out
that, considered as one whole, it still seems lacking
in any of that living sense of the state out of which
constructive effort must arise, and that, conse-
quently, enormous amounts of energy go to waste
in anarchistic and chaotically competitive private
enterprise. I believe there are powerful forces at
work in the trend of modern thought, science, and
method, in the direction of bringing order, control,
and design into this confused gigantic conflict, and
the discussion of these constructive forces must
necessarily form the crown of my forecast of America's future. But before I come to that I must deal
with certain American traits that puzzle me, that I
cannot completely explain to myself, that dash my
large expectations with an obstinate shadow of foreboding. Essentially these are disintegrating in-

fluences, in the nature of a fierce intolerance, that lead to conflicts and destroy co-operation. One makes one's criticism with compunction. One moves through the American world, meeting constantly with kindness and hospitality, with a familiar helpfulness that is delightful, with sympathetic enterprise and energetic imagination, and then suddenly there flashes out a quality of harshness. . . .

I will explain in a few minutes what I mean by this flash of harshness. Let me confess here that I cannot determine whether it is a necessary consequence of American conditions, the scar upon the soul of too strenuous business competition, or whether it is something deeper, some subtle, unavoidable infection perhaps in this soil that was once the Red Indian's battle-ground, some poison, it may be, mingled with this clear exhilarating air. And going with this harshness there seems also something else, a contempt for abstract justice that one does not find in any European intelligence—not even among the English. This contempt may be a correlative of the intense practicality begotten by a scruple-destroying commercial training. That, at any rate, is my own prepossession. Conceivably I am over-disposed to make that tall lady in New York Harbor stand as a symbol for the liberty of property, and to trace the indisputable hastiness of life here—it is haste sometimes rather than speed,—its scorn of æsthetic and abstract issues, this frequent quality of harshness, and a certain public disorder, whatever indeed mars the splendid promise and youth of America, to that. I think it is an accident of the commercial phase that presses men beyond dignity, patience, and magnanimity. I am loath to believe it is something fundamentally American.

I have very clearly in my memory the figure of young MacQueen, in his gray prison clothes in Trenton jail, and how I talked with him. He and Mr. Booker T. Washington and Maxim Gorky stand for me as figures in the shadow—symbolical men. I think of America as pride and promise, as large growth and large courage, all set with beautiful fluttering bunting, and then my vision of these three men comes back to me; they return presences inseparable from my American effect, unlit and uncomplaining on the sunless side of her, implying rather than voicing certain accusations. America can be hasty, can be obstinately thoughtless and unjust. . . .

Well, let me set down as shortly as I can how I saw them, and then go on again with my main thesis.

II

MacQueen is one of those young men
MacQueen England is now making by the thousand in her elementary schools—a man of that active, intelligent, mentally hungry, self-educating sort that is giving us our elementary teach-

ers, our labor members, able journalists, authors, civil servants, and some of the most public-spirited and efficient of our municipal administrators. He is the sort of man an Englishman grows prouder of as he sees America and something of her politicians and labor leaders. After his board - school days MacQueen went to work as a painter and grainer, and gave his spare energy to self-education. He mastered German, and read widely and freely. He corresponded with William Morris, devoured Tolstoy and Bernard Shaw, followed the *Clarion* week by week, discussed social questions, wrote to the newspapers, debated, made speeches. The English reader will begin to recognize the type. Jail had worn him when I saw him, but I should think he was always physically delicate; he wears spectacles, he warms emotionally as he talks. And he decided, after much excogitation, that the ideal state is one of so fine a quality of moral training that people will not need coercion and repressive laws. He calls himself an anarchist—of the early Christian, Tolstoyan, non-resisting school. Such an anarchist was Emerson, among other dead Americans whose names are better treasured than their thoughts. That sort of anarchist has as much connection with embittered bomb-throwers and assassins as Miss Florence Nightingale has with the woman Hartmann, who put on a nurse's uniform to poison and rob. . . .

Well, MacQueen led an active life in England, married, made a decent living, and took an honorable part in the local affairs of Leeds until he was twenty-six. Then he conceived a desire for wider opportunity than England offers men of his class.

In January, 1902, he crossed the Atlantic, and, no doubt, he came very much aglow with the American idea. He felt that he was exchanging a decadent country of dwarfing social and political traditions for a land of limitless outlook. He became a proof-reader in New York, and began to seek around him for opportunities of speaking and forwarding social progress. He tried to float a newspaper. The New York labor-unions found him a useful speaker, and, among others, the German silk-workers of New York became aware of him. In June they asked him to go to Paterson to speak in German to the weavers in that place.

The silk-dyers were on strike in Paterson, but the weavers were weaving "scab-silk," dyed by dyers elsewhere, and it was believed that the dyers' strike would fail unless they struck also. They had to be called out. They were chiefly Italians, some Hungarians. It was felt by the New York German silk-workers that perhaps MacQueen's German learned in England might meet the linguistic difficulties of the case.

He went. I hope he will forgive me if I say that his was an extremely futile expedition. He did very little. He wrote an entirely harmless article or so in English for *La Questione Sociale*, and he declined with horror and publicity to appear upon the same platform with a mischievous and violent lady anarchist called Emma Goldman. On June 17, 1902, he went to Paterson again, and spoke to his own undoing. There is no evidence that he said anything illegal or inflammatory, there is clear evidence that he bored his audience. They shouted him down, and called for a prominent local speaker named Galiano. MacQueen subsided into the background, and Galiano spoke for an hour in Italian. He aroused great enthusiasm, and the proceedings terminated with a destructive riot.

Eight witnesses testify to the ineffectual efforts on the part of MacQueen to combat the violence in progress. . . .

That finishes the story of MacQueen's activities in America, for which he is now in durance at Trenton. He, in common with a large crowd and in common, too, with nearly all the witnesses against him, did commit one offence against the law—he did not go home when destruction began. He was arrested next day. From that time forth his fate was out of his hands, and in the control of a number of people who wanted to "make an example" of the Paterson strikers. The press took up MacQueen. They began to clothe the bare bones of this simple little history I have told in fluent, unmitigated lying. They blackened him, one might think, out of sheer artistic pleasure in the operation. They called this rather nervous, educated, nobly meaning if ill-advised young man a "notorious anarchist"; his

head - line title became "Anarchistic MacQueen";
they wrote his "story" in a vein of imaginative
fervor; they invented "an unsavory police record"
for him in England; and enlarged upon the marvellous secret organization for crime of which he was
representative and leader. In a little while Mac-
Queen had ceased to be a credible human being; he
might have been invented by Mr. William le Queux.
He was arrested—Galiano went scot-free—and released on bail. It was discovered that his pleasant,
decent Yorkshire wife and three children were
coming out to America to him, and she became "the
woman Nellie Barton"—her maiden name—and "a
socialist of the Emma Goldman stripe." This, one
gathers, is the most horrible stripe known to American journalism. Had there been a worse one, Mrs.
MacQueen would have been the *ex officio*. And now
here is an extraordinary thing—public officials began
to join in the process. This is what perplexes me most
in this affair. I am told that Assistant-Secretary-of-
the-Treasury H. A. Taylor, without a fact to go upon,
subscribed to the "unsavory record" legend and
Assistant-Secretary C. H. Keep fell in with it. They
must have seen what it was they were indorsing.
In a letter from Mr. Keep to the Reverend A. W.
Wishart, of Trenton (who throughout has fought
most gallantly for justice in this case), I find Mr.
Keep distinguishes himself by the artistic device of
putting "William MacQueen's" name in inverted
commas. So, very delicately, he conveys out of the

void the insinuation that the name is an alias. Meanwhile the Commissioner of Immigration prepared to
take a hand in the game of breaking up MacQueen.
He stopped Mrs. MacQueen at the threshold of
liberty, imprisoned her in Ellis Island, and sent her
back to Europe. MacQueen, still on bail, was not
informed of this action, and waited on the pier for
some hours before he understood. His wife had
come second class to America, but she was returned
first class, and the steamship company seized her
goods for the return fare. . . .

That was more than MacQueen could stand. He
had been tried, convicted, sentenced to five years'
imprisonment, and he was now out on bail pending
an appeal. Anxiety about his wife and children was
too much for him. He slipped off to England after
them ("Escape of the Anarchist MacQueen"), made
what provision and arrangements he could for them,
and returned in time to save his bondsman's money
("Capture of the Escaped Anarchist MacQueen").
Several members of the Leeds City Council ("Criminal Associates in Europe") saw him off. That was
in 1903. His appeal had been refused on a technical
point. He went into Trenton jail, and there he is
to this day. There I saw him. Trenton Jail did not
impress me as an agreeable place. The building is
fairly old, and there is no nonsense about the food.
The cells hold, some of them, four criminals, some of
them two, but latterly MacQueen has had spells in
the infirmary, and has managed to get a cell to him-

self. Many of the criminals are negroes and half-breeds, imprisoned for unspeakable offences. In the exercising-yard MacQueen likes to keep apart. "When I first came I used to get in a corner," he said. . . .

Now this case of MacQueen has exercised my mind enormously. It was painful to go out of the gray jail again after I had talked to him—of Shaw and Morris, of the Fabian Society and the British labor members—into sunlight and freedom, and ever and again, as I went about New York having the best of times among the most agreeable people, the figure of him would come back to me quite vividly, in his gray dress, sitting on the edge of an unaccustomed chair, hands on his knees, speaking a little nervously and jerkily, and very glad indeed to see me. He is younger than myself, but much my sort of man, and we talked of books and education and his case like brothers. There can be no doubt to any sensible person who will look into the story of his conviction, who will even go and see him, that there has been a serious miscarriage of justice.

There has been a serious miscarriage of justice, such as (unhappily) might happen in any country. That is nothing distinctive of America. But what does impress me as remarkable and perplexing is the immense difficulty — the perhaps unsurmountable difficulty—of getting this man released. The Governor of the State of New Jersey knows he is innocent, the judges of the Court of Pardons know he is innocent. Three of them I was able to button-hole at Trenton, and hear their point of view. Two are of the minority and for release, one was doubtful in attitude but hostile in spirit. They hold, the man, he thinks, on the score of public policy. They put it that Paterson is a "hotbed" of crime and violence; that once MacQueen is released every anarchist in the country will be emboldened to crime, and so on and so on. I admit Paterson festers, but if we are to punish anybody instead of reforming the system, it's the masters who ought to be in jail for that.

"What will the property-owners in Paterson say to us if this man is released?" one of the judges admitted frankly.

"But he hadn't anything to do with the violence," I said, an argued the case over again—quite missing the point of that objection.

Whenever I had a chance in New York, in Boston, in Washington, even amid the conversation of a Washington dinner-table, I dragged up the case of MacQueen. Nobody seemed indignant. One lady admitted the sentence was heavy, "he might have been given six months to cool off in," she said. I protested he ought not to have been given a day. "Why did he go there?" said a Supreme Court judge in Washington, a lawyer in New York, and several other people. "Wasn't he making trouble?" I was asked.

At last that reached my sluggish intelligence.

Yet I still hesitate to accept the new interpretations. Galiano, who preached blind violence and made the riot, got off scot-free; MacQueen, who wanted a legitimate strike on British lines, went to jail. So long as the social injustice, the sweated disorder of Paterson's industrialism, vents its cries in Italian in *La Questione Sociale*, so long as it remains an inaudible misery so far as the great public is concerned, making vehement yet impotent appeals to mere force, and so losing its last chances of popular sympathy, American property, I gather, is content. The masters and the immigrants can deal with one another on those lines. But to have outsiders coming in!

There is an active press campaign against the release of "the Anarchist MacQueen," and I do not believe that Mr. Wishart will succeed in his endeavors. I think MacQueen will serve out his five years.

The plain truth is that no one pretends he is in jail on his merits; he is in jail as an example and lesson to any one who proposes to come between master and immigrant worker in Paterson. He has attacked the system. The people who profit by the system, the people who think things are "all right as they are," have hit back in the most effectual way they can, according to their lights.

That, I think, accounts for the sustained quality of the lying in this case, and, indeed, for the whole situation. He is in jail on principle and without personal animus, just as they used to tar and feather the stray abolitionist on principle in Carolina. The policy of stringent discouragement is a reasonable one — scoundrelly, no doubt, but understandable. And I think I can put myself sufficiently into the place of the Paterson masters, of the Trenton judges, of those journalists, of those subordinate officials at Washington even, to understand their motives and inducements. I indulge in no self-righteous pride. Simply, I thank Heaven I have not had their peculiar temptations.

But my riddle lies in the attitude of the public—of the American nation, which hasn't, it seems, a spark of moral indignation for this sort of thing, which indeed joins in quite cheerfully against the victim.

It is ill served by its press, no doubt, but surely it understands. . . .

III

THEN I assisted at the coming of Maxim Gorky, and witnessed many intimate details of what Professor Giddings, that courageous publicist, has called his "lynching."

Here, again, is a case I fail altogether to understand. The surface values of that affair have a touch of the preposterous. I set them down in infinite perplexity.

My first week in New York was in the period of

Gorky's advent. Expectation was at a high pitch, and one might have foretold a stupendous, a history-making campaign. The American nation seemed concentrated upon one great and ennobling idea, the freedom of Russia, and upon Gorky as the embodiment of that idea. A protest was to be made against cruelty and violence and massacre. That great figure of Liberty with the torch was to make it flare visibly half-way round the world, reproving tyranny.

Gorky arrived, and the *éclat* was immense. We dined him, we lunched him, we were photographed in his company by flash-light. I very gladly shared that honor, for Gorky is not only a great master of the art I practise, but a splendid personality. He is one of those people to whom the camera does no justice, whose work, as I know it in an English translation, forceful as it is, fails very largely to convey his peculiar quality. His is a big, quiet figure; there is a curious power of appeal in his face, a large simplicity in his voice and gesture. He was dressed, when I met him, in peasant clothing, in a belted blue shirt, trousers of some shiny black material, and boots; and save for a few common greetings he has no other language than Russian. So it was necessary that he should bring with him some one he could trust to interpret him to the world. And having, too, much of the practical helplessness of his type of genius, he could not come without his right hand, that brave and honorable lady, Madame Andreieva, who has been now for years in every-

thing but the severest legal sense his wife. Russia
has no Dakota; and although his legal wife has
long since found another companion, the Orthodox
Church in Russia has no divorce facilities for men in
the revolutionary camp. So Madame Andreieva
stands to him as George Eliot stood to George Lewes,
and I suppose the two of them had almost forgotten
the technical illegality of their tie, until it burst upon
them and the American public in a monstrous storm
of exposure.

It was like a summer thunder-storm. At one moment Gorky was in an immense sunshine, a plenipo-
tentiary from oppression to liberty, at the next he
was being almost literally pelted through the streets.

I do not know what motive actuated a certain
section of the American press to initiate this pelting
of Maxim Gorky. A passion for moral purity may
perhaps have prompted it, but certainly no passion
for purity ever before begot so brazen and abundant
a torrent of lies. It was precisely the sort of campaign that damned poor MacQueen, but this time
on an altogether imperial scale. The irregularity
of Madame Andreieva's position was a mere point of
departure. The journalists went on to invent a
deserted wife and children, they declared Madame
Andreieva was an "actress," and loaded her with
all the unpleasant implications of that unfortunate
word; they spoke of her generally as "the woman
Andreieva"; they called upon the Commissioner of
Immigration to deport her as a "female of bad

character"; quite influential people wrote to him
to that effect; they published the name of the hotel
that sheltered her, and organized a boycott. Whoever dared to countenance the victims was de-
nounced. Professor Dewar of Columbia had given
them a reception; "Dewar must go," said the head-
lines. Mark Twain, who had assisted in the great
welcome, was invited to recant and contribute un-
friendly comments. The Gorkys were pursued with
insult from hotel to hotel. Hotel after hotel turned
them out. They found themselves at last, after midnight, in the streets of New York city with every
door closed against them. Infected persons could
not have been treated more abominably in a town
smitten with a panic of plague.

This change happened in the course of twenty-
four hours. On one day Gorky was at the zenith,
on the next he had been swept from the world. To
me it was astounding—it was terrifying. I wanted
to talk to Gorky about it, to find out the hidden
springs of this amazing change. I spent a Sunday
evening looking for him with an ever-deepening
respect for the power of the American press. I had
a quaint conversation with the clerk of the hotel in
Fifth Avenue from which he had first been driven.
Europeans can scarcely hope to imagine the moral
altitudes at which American hotels are conducted.
. . . I went thence to seek Mr. Abraham Cahan in the
East Side, and thence to other people I knew, but in
vain. Gorky was obliterated.

I thought this affair was a whirlwind of foolish mis-
understanding, such as may happen in any capital,
and that presently his entirely tolerable relationship
would be explained. But for all the rest of my time
in New York this insensate campaign went on.
There was no attempt of any importance to stem the
tide, and to this day large sections of the American
public must be under the impression that this great
writer is a depraved man of pleasure accompanied by
a favorite cocotte. The writers of paragraphs rack-
ed their brains to invent new and smart ways of in-
sulting Madame Andreieva. The chaste entertainers
of the music-halls of the Tenderloin district introduced allusions. And amid this riot of personalities Russia was forgotten. The massacres, the chaos
of cruelty and blundering, the tyranny, the women
outraged, the children tortured and slain—all that
was forgotten. In Boston, in Chicago, it was the
same. At the bare suggestion of Gorky's coming
the same outbreak occurred, the same display of im-
becile gross lying, the same absolute disregard of the
tragic cause he had come to plead.

One gleam of comedy in this remarkable outbreak I
recall. Some one in ineffectual protest had asked
what Americans would have said if Benjamin
Franklin had encountered such ignominies on his
similar mission of appeal to Paris before the War of
Independence. "Benjamin Franklin," retorted one
bright young Chicago journalist, "was a man of very
different moral character from Gorky," and proceed-

ed to explain how Chicago was prepared to defend
the purity of her homes against the invader. Benjamin Franklin, it is true, *was* a person of very different morals from Gorky—but I don't think that
bright young man in Chicago had a very sound idea
of where the difference lay.

I spent my last evening on American soil in the
hospitable home in Staten Island that sheltered
Gorky and Madame Andreieva. After dinner we
sat together in the deepening twilight upon a broad
veranda that looks out upon one of the most beautiful
views in the world, upon serene large spaces of land
and sea, upon slopes of pleasant, window-lit, tree-set
wooden houses, upon the glittering clusters of lights,
and the black and luminous shipping that comes and
goes about the Narrows and the Upper Bay. Half
masked by a hill contour to the left was the light
of the torch of Liberty. . . . Gorky's big form fell into
shadow, Madame Andreieva sat at his feet, translating methodically, sentence by sentence, into clear
French whatever he said, translating our speeches
into Russian. He told us stories—of the soul of the
Russian, of Russian religious sects, of kindnesses and
cruelties, of his great despair.

Ever and again, in the pauses, my eyes would go
to where New York far away glittered like a brighter
and more numerous Pleiades.

I gauged something of the real magnitude of this
one man's disappointment, the immense expectation
of his arrival, the impossible dream of his mission

13   183

He had come—the Russian peasant in person, out of a terrific confusion of bloodshed, squalor, injustice—to tell America, the land of light and achieved freedom, of all these evil things. She would receive him, help him, understand truly what he meant with his "Rossia." I could imagine how he had felt as he came in the big steamer to her, up that large converging display of space and teeming energy. There she glowed to-night across the water, a queen among cities, as if indeed she was the light of the world. Nothing, I think, can ever rob that splendid harbor approach of its invincible quality of promise. . . . And to him she had shown herself no more than the luminous hive of multitudes of base and busy, greedy and childish little men.

MacQueen in jail, Gorky with his reputation wantonly bludgeoned and flung aside; they are just two chance specimens of the myriads who have come up this great waterway bearing hope and gifts.

CHAPTER XII

THE TRAGEDY OF COLOR

I

I seem to find the same hastiness and
something of the same note of harshness that strike me in the cases of Mac-
Queen and Gorky in America's treatment of her
colored population. I am aware how intricate, how
multitudinous, the aspects of this enormous question
have become, but looking at it in the broad and
transitory manner I have proposed for myself in
these papers, it does seem to present many parallel
elements. There is the same disposition towards an
indiscriminating verdict, the same disregard of proportion as between small evils and great ones, the
same indifference to the fact that the question does
not stand alone, but is a part, and this time a by no
means small part, in the working out of America's
destinies.

In regard to the colored population, just as in
regard to the great and growing accumulations of
unassimilated and increasingly unpopular Jews, and
to the great and growing multitudes of Roman

*Harsh Judg-
ments*

Catholics whose special education contradicts at so many points those conceptions of individual judgment and responsibility upon which America relies, I have attempted time after time to get some answer from the Americans I have met to what is to me the most obvious of questions. "Your grandchildren and the grandchildren of these people will have to live in this country side by side; do you propose, do you believe it possible, that under the increasing pressure of population and competition they should be living then in just the same relations that you and these people are living now; if you do not, then what relations do you propose shall exist between them?"

It is not too much to say that I have never once had the beginnings of an answer to this question. Usually one is told with great gravity that the problem of color is one of the most difficult that we have to consider, and the conversation then breaks up into discursive anecdotes and statements about black people. One man will dwell upon the uncontrollable violence of a black man's evil passions (in Jamaica and Barbadoes colored people form an overwhelming proportion of the population, and they have behaved in an exemplary fashion for the last thirty years); another will dilate upon the incredible stupidity of the full-blooded negro (during my stay in New York the prize for oratory at Columbia University, oratory which was the one redeeming charm of Daniel Webster, was awarded to a Zulu of unmitigated blackness); a third will speak of his physical offensiveness, his peculiar smell which necessitates his social isolation (most well-to-do Southerners are brought up by negro "mammies"); others, again, will enter upon the painful history of the years that followed the war, though it seems a foolish thing to let those wrongs of the past dominate the outlook for the future. And one charming Southern lady expressed the attitude of mind of a whole class very completely, I think, when she said, "You have to be one of us to feel this question at all as it ought to be felt."

There, I think, I got something tangible. These emotions are a cult.

My globe-trotting impudence will seem, no doubt, to mount to its zenith when I declare that hardly any Americans at all seem to be in possession of the elementary facts in relation to this question. These broad facts are not taught, as of course they ought to be taught, in school; and what each man knows is picked up by the accidents of his own untrained observation, by conversation always tinctured by personal prejudice, by hastily read newspapers and magazine articles and the like. The quality of this discussion is very variable, but on the whole pretty low. While I was in New York opinion was greatly swayed by an article in, if I remember rightly, the *Century Magazine*, by a gentleman who had deduced from a few weeks' observation in the slums of Khartoum the entire incapacity of the negro to establish a civilization of his own. He never had, therefore he never could; a discouraging ratiocination. We English, a century or so ago, said all these things of the native Irish. If there is any trend of opinion at all in this matter at present, it lies in the direction of a generous decision on the part of the North and West to leave the black more and more to the judgment and mercy of the white people with whom he is locally associated. This judgment and mercy points, on the whole, to an accentuation of the colored man's natural inferiority, to the cessation of any other educational attempts than those that increase his industrial usefulness (it is already illegal in Louisiana to educate him above a contemptible level), to his industrial exploitation through usury and legal chicanery, and to a systematic strengthening of the social barriers between colored people of whatever shade and the whites.

Meanwhile, in this state of general confusion, in the absence of any determining rules or assumptions, all sorts of things are happening—according to the accidents of local feeling. In Massachusetts you have people with, I am afraid, an increasing sense of sacrifice to principle, lunching and dining with people of color. They do it less than they did, I was told. Massachusetts stands, I believe, at the top of the scale of tolerant humanity. One seems to reach the bottom at Springfield, Missouri, which is a county seat with a college, an academy, a high school, and a zoological garden. There the exemplary method reaches the nadir. Last April three unfortunate negroes were burned to death, apparently because they were negroes, and as a general corrective of impertinence. They seem to have been innocent of any particular offence. It was a sort of racial sacrament. The edified Sunday-school children hurried from their gospel-teaching to search for souvenirs among the ashes, and competed with great spirit for a fragment of charred skull.

It is true that in this latter case Governor Folk acted with vigor and justice, and that the better element of Springfield society was evidently shocked when it was found that quite innocent negroes had been used in these instructive pyrotechnics; but the fact remains that a large and numerically important section of the American public does think that fierce and cruel reprisals are a necessary part of the system of relationships between white and colored man. In our dispersed British community we have almost exactly the same range between our better attitudes and our worse—I'm making no claim of national superiority. In London, perhaps, we outdo Massachusetts in liberality; in the National Liberal Club or the Reform a black man meets all the courtesies of humanity—as though there was no such thing as color. But, on the other hand, the Cape won't bear looking into for a moment. The same conditions give the same results; a half-educated white population of British or Dutch or German ingredients greedy for gain, ill controlled and feebly influenced, in contact with a black population,

is bound to reproduce the same brutal and stupid
aggressions, the same half - honest prejudices to
justify those aggressions, the same ugly, mean
excuses. "Things are better in Jamaica and Barbadoes," said I, in a moment of patriotic weakness,
to Mr. Booker T. Washington.

"Eh!" said he, and thought in that long silent
way he has. . . . "They're worse in South Africa—
much. Here we've got a sort of light. We know
generally what we've got to stand. *There*—"

His words sent my memory back to some conversations I had quite recently with a man from a
dry-goods store in Johannesburg. He gave me
clearly enough the attitude of the common white out
there; the dull prejudice; the readiness to take advantage of the "boy"; the utter disrespect for
colored womankind; the savage, intolerant resentment, dashed dangerously with fear, which the native
arouses in him. (Think of all that must have happened in wrongful practice and wrongful law and
neglected educational possibilities before our Zulus
in Natal were goaded to face massacre, spear against
rifle!) The rare and culminating result of education
and experience is to enable men to grasp facts, to
balance justly among their fluctuating and innumerable aspects, and only a small minority in our world
is educated to that pitch. Ignorant people can
think only in types and abstractions, can achieve
only emphatic absolute decisions, and when the
commonplace American or the commonplace colonial

Briton sets to work to "think over" the negro problem, he instantly banishes most of the material evidence from his mind—clears for action, as it were. He forgets the genial carriage of the ordinary colored man, his beaming face, his kindly eye, his rich, jolly voice, his touching and trusted friendliness, his amiable, unprejudiced readiness to serve and follow a white man who seems to know what he is doing. He forgets—perhaps he has never seen—the dear humanity of these people, their slightly exaggerated vanity, their innocent and delightful love of color and song, their immense capacity for affection, the warm romantic touch in their imaginations. He ignores the real fineness of the indolence that despises servile toil, of the carelessness that disdains the watchful aggressive economies, day by day, now a wretched little gain here and now a wretched little gain there, that make the dirty fortune of the Russian Jews who prey upon color in the Carolinas. No; in the place of all these tolerable every-day experiences he lets his imagination go to work upon a monster, the "real nigger."

"Ah! You don't know the *real* nigger," said one American to me when I praised the colored people I had seen. "You should see the buck nigger down South, Congo brand. Then you'd understand, sir."

His voice, his face had a gleam of passionate animosity.

One could see he had been brooding himself out of all relations to reality in this matter. He was a

man beyond reason or pity. He was obsessed.
Hatred of that imaginary diabolical "buck nigger"
blackened his soul. It was no good to talk to him
of the "buck American, Packingtown brand," or the
"buck Englishman, suburban race-meeting type,"
and to ask him if these intensely disagreeable persons
justified outrages on Senator Lodge, let us say, or
Mrs. Longworth. No reply would have come from
him. "You don't understand the question," he
would have answered. "You don't know how we
Southerners feel."

Well, one can make a tolerable guess.

II

I CERTAINLY did not begin to realize
The White
Strain
one most important aspect of this
question until I reached America. I
thought of those eight millions as of men, black as
ink. But when I met Mr. Booker T. Washington,
for example, I met a man certainly as white in appearance as our Admiral Fisher, who is, as a matter
of fact, quite white. A very large proportion of
these colored people, indeed, is more than half white.
One hears a good deal about the high social origins
of the Southern planters, very many derive indisputably from the first families of England. It is the
same blood flows in these mixed colored people's
veins. Just think of the sublime absurdity, therefore, of the ban. There are gentlemen of education

and refinement, qualified lawyers and doctors, whose ancestors assisted in the Norman Conquest, and they dare not enter a car marked "white" and intrude upon the dignity of the rising loan-monger from Esthonia. For them the "Jim Crow" car. . . .

One tries to put that aspect to the American in vain. "These people," you say, "are nearer your blood, nearer your temper, than any of those bright-eyed, ringleted immigrants on the East Side. Are you ashamed of your poor relations? Even if you don't like the half, or the quarter of negro blood, you might deal civilly with the three-quarters white. It doesn't say much for your faith in your own racial prepotency, anyhow." . . .

The answer to that is usually in terms of mania.

"Let me tell you a little story just to illustrate," said one deponent to me in an impressive undertone—" just to illustrate, you know. . . . A few years ago a young fellow came to Boston from New Orleans. Looked all right. Dark—but he explained that by an Italian grandmother. Touch of French in him, too. Popular. Well, he made advances to a Boston girl—good family. Gave a fairly straight account of himself. Married."

He paused. "Course of time—offspring. Little son."

His eye made me feel what was coming.

"Was it by any chance very, very black?" I whispered.

"Yes, *sir*. Black! Black as your hat. Abso-

193

lutely negroid. Projecting jaw, thick lips, frizzy hair, flat nose—everything. . . .

"But consider the mother's feelings, sir, consider that! A pure-minded, pure white woman!"

What can one say to a story of this sort, when the taint in the blood surges up so powerfully as to blacken the child at birth beyond even the habit of the pure-blooded negro? What can you do with a public opinion made of this class of ingredient? And this story of the lamentable results of intermarriage was used, not as an argument against intermarriage, but as an argument against the extension of quite rudimentary civilities to the men of color. "If you eat with them, you've got to marry them," he said, an entirely fabulous post-prandial responsibility.

It is to the tainted whites my sympathies go out. The black or mainly black people seem to be fairly content with their inferiority; one sees them all about the States as waiters, cab-drivers, railway porters, car attendants, laborers of various sorts, a pleasant, smiling, acquiescent folk. But consider the case of a man with a broader brain than such small uses need, conscious, perhaps, of exceptional gifts, capable of wide interests and sustained attempts, who is perhaps as English as you or I, with just a touch of color in his eyes, in his lips, in his finger-nails, and in his imagination. Think of the accumulating sense of injustice he must bear with him through life, the perpetual slight and insult he must undergo from all that is vulgar and brutal among the whites! Something of that one may read in the sorrowful pages of Du Bois's *The Souls of Black Folk.* They would have made Alexandre Dumas travel in the Jim Crow car if he had come to Virginia. But I can imagine some sort of protest on the part of that admirable but extravagant man. . . . They even talk of "Jim Crow elevators" now in Southern hotels.

At Hull House, in Chicago, I was present at a conference of colored people—Miss Jane Addams efficiently in control—to consider the coming of a vexatious play, "The Clansman," which seems to have been written and produced entirely to exacerbate racial feeling. Both men and women were present, business people, professional men, and their wives; the speaking was clear, temperate, and wonderfully to the point, high above the level of any British town council I have ever attended. One lady would have stood out as capable and charming in any sort of public discussion in England—though we are not wanting in good women speakers—and she was at least three-quarters black. . . .

And while I was in Chicago, too, I went to the Peking Theatre — a "coon" music-hall — and saw something of a lower level of colored life. The common white, I must explain, delights in calling colored people "coons," and the negro, so far as I could learn, uses no retaliatory word. It was a "variety" entertainment, with one turn, at least, of quite distinguished merit, good-humored and brisk throughout. I watched keenly, and I could detect nothing of that trail of base suggestion one would find as a matter of course in a music-hall in such English towns as Brighton and Portsmouth. What one heard of kissing and love-making was quite artless and simple indeed. The negro, it seemed to me, did this sort of thing with a better grace and a better temper than a Londoner, and shows, I think, a finer self-respect. He thinks more of deportment, he bears himself more elegantly by far than the white at the same social level. The audience reminded me of the sort of gathering one would find in a theatre in Camden Town or Hoxton. There were a number of family groups, the girls brightly dressed, and young couples quite of the London music-hall type. Clothing ran "smart," but not smarter than it would be among fairly prosperous north London Jews. There was no gallery —socially—no collection of orange-eating, interrupting hooligans at all. Nobody seemed cross, nobody seemed present for vicious purposes, and everybody was sober. Indeed, there and elsewhere I took and confirmed a mighty liking to these gentle, human, dark-skinned people.

III

BUT whatever aspect I recall of this
Mr. Booker T. Washington great taboo that shows no signs of
lifting, of this great problem of the
future that America in her haste, her indiscriminat-

ing prejudice, her lack of any sustained study and
teaching of the broad issues she must decide, com-
plicates and intensifies, and makes threatening,
there presently comes back to mind the browned
face of Mr. Booker T. Washington, as he talked to
me over our lunch in Boston.

He has a face rather Irish in type, and the soft
slow negro voice. He met my regard with the
brown sorrowful eyes of his race. He wanted very
much that I should hear him make a speech, because
then his words came better; he talked, he implied,
with a certain difficulty. But I preferred to have
his talking, and get not the orator—every one tells
me he is an altogether great orator in this country
where oratory is still esteemed—but the man.

He answered my questions meditatively. I wanted to know with an active pertinacity. What
struck me most was the way in which his sense of the
overpowering forces of race prejudice weighs upon
him. It is a thing he accepts; in our time and conditions it is not to be fought about. He makes one
feel with an exaggerated intensity (though I could
not even draw him to admit) its monstrous injustice.
He makes no accusations. He is for taking it as a
part of the present fate of his "people," and for
doing all that can be done for them within the limit
it sets.

Therein he differs from Du Bois, the other great
spokesman color has found in our time. Du Bois,
is more of the artist, less of the statesman; he con-

ceals his passionate resentment all too thinly. He batters himself into rhetoric against these walls. He will not repudiate the clear right of the black man to every educational facility, to equal citizenship, and equal respect. But Mr. Washington has statecraft. He looks before and after, and plans and keeps his counsel with the scope and range of a statesman. I use "statesman" in its highest sense; his is a mind that can grasp the situation and destinies of a people. After I had talked to him I went back to my club, and found there an English newspaper with a report of the opening debate upon Mr. Birrell's Education Bill. It was like turning from the discussion of life and death to a dispute about the dregs in the bottom of a tea-cup somebody had neglected to wash up in Victorian times.

I argued strongly against the view he seems to hold that black and white might live without mingling and without injustice, side by side. That I do not believe. Racial differences seem to me always to exasperate intercourse unless people have been elaborately trained to ignore them. Uneducated men are as bad as cattle in persecuting all that is different among themselves. The most miserable and disorderly countries of the world are the countries where two races, two inadequate cultures, keep a jarring, continuous separation. "You must repudiate separation," I said. "No peoples have ever yet endured the tension of intermingled distinctness."

"May we not become a peculiar people—like the Jews?" he suggested. "Isn't that possible?"

But there I could not agree with him. I thought of the dreadful history of the Jews and Armenians. And the negro cannot do what the Jews and Armenians have done. The colored people of America are of a different quality from the Jew altogether, more genial, more careless, more sympathetic, franker, less intellectual, less acquisitive, less wary and restrained—in a word, more Occidental. They have no common religion and culture, no conceit of race to hold them together. The Jews make a ghetto for themselves wherever they go; no law but their own solidarity has given America the East Side. The colored people are ready to disperse and interbreed, are not a community at all in the Jewish sense, but outcasts from a community. They are the victims of a prejudice that has to be destroyed. These things I urged, but it was, I think, empty speech to my hearer. I could talk lightly of destroying that prejudice, but he knew better. It is the central fact of his life, a law of his being. He has shaped all his projects and policy upon that. Exclusion is inevitable. So he dreams of a colored race of decent and inaggressive men silently giving the lie to all the legend of their degradation. They will have their own doctors, their own lawyers, their own capitalists, their own banks—because the whites desire it so. But will the uneducated whites endure even so submissive a vindication as that? Will they suffer the horrid spectacle of free and self-satisfied negroes in decent clothing on any terms without resentment?

He explained how at the Tuskegee Institute they make useful men, skilled engineers, skilled agriculturalists, men to live down the charge of practical incompetence, of ignorant and slovenly farming and house management. . . .

"I wish you would tell me," I said, abruptly, "just what you think of the attitude of white America towards you. Do you think it is generous?"

He regarded me for a moment. "No end of people help us," he said.

"Yes," I said; "but the ordinary man. Is he fair?"

"Some things are not fair," he said, leaving the general question alone. "It isn't fair to refuse a colored man a berth on a sleeping-car. I?—I happen to be a privileged person, they make an exception for me; but the ordinary educated colored man isn't admitted to a sleeping-car at all. If he has to go a long journey, he has to sit up all night. His white competitor sleeps. Then in some places, in the hotels and restaurants— It's all right here in Boston—but southwardly he can't get proper refreshments. All that's a handicap. . . .

"The remedy lies in education," he said; "ours— *and theirs.*

"The real thing," he told me, "isn't to be done by talking and agitation. It's a matter of lives. The only answer to it all is for colored men to be patient, to make themselves competent, to do good work, to live well, to give no occasion against us. We feel that. In a way it's an inspiration. . . .

"There is a man here in Boston, a negro, who owns and runs some big stores, employs all sorts of people, deals justly. That man has done more good for our people than all the eloquence or argument in the world. . . . That is what we have to do—it is all we *can* do." . . .

Whatever America has to show in heroic living to-day, I doubt if she can show anything finer than the quality of the resolve, the steadfast effort hundreds of black and colored men are making to-day to live blamelessly, honorably, and patiently, getting for themselves what scraps of refinement, learning, and beauty they may, keeping their hold on a civilization they are grudged and denied. They do it not for themselves only, but for all their race. Each educated colored man is an ambassador to civilization. They know they have a handicap, that they are not exceptionally brilliant nor clever people. Yet every such man stands, one likes to think, aware of his representative and vicarious character, fighting against foul imaginations, misrepresentations, injustice, insult, and the naïve unspeakable meannesses of base antagonists. Every one of them who keeps decent and honorable does a little to beat that opposition down.

But the patience the negro needs! He may not

even look contempt. He must admit superiority in those whose daily conduct to him is the clearest evidence of moral inferiority. We sympathetic whites, indeed, may claim honor for him; if he is wise he will be silent under our advocacy. He must go to and fro self-controlled, bereft of all the equalities that the great flag of America proclaims—that flag for whose united empire his people fought and died, giving place and precedence to the strangers who pour in to share its beneficence, strangers ignorant even of its tongue. That he must do—and wait. The Welsh, the Irish, the Poles, the white South, the indefatigable Jews may cherish grievances and rail aloud. He must keep still. They may be hysterical revengeful, threatening, and perverse; their wrongs excuse them. For him there is no excuse. And of all the races upon earth, which has suffered such wrongs as this negro blood that is still imputed to him as a sin? These people who disdain him, who have no sense of reparation towards him, have sinned against him beyond all measure. . . .

No, I can't help idealizing the dark submissive figure of the negro in this spectacle of America. He, too, seems to me to sit waiting—and waiting with a marvellous and simple-minded patience—for finer understandings and a nobler time.

CHAPTER XIII

THE MIND OF A MODERN STATE

I

I DO not know if I am conveying to
_{Recapitulatory} any extent the picture of America as I
see it, the vast rich various continent,
the gigantic energetic process of development, the
acquisitive successes, the striving failures, the multitudes of those rising and falling who come between,
all set in a texture of spacious countryside, animate
with pleasant timber homes, of clangorous towns
that bristle to the skies, of great exploitation dis-
tricts and crowded factories, of wide deserts and
mine-torn mountains, and huge half-tamed rivers.
I have tried to make the note of immigration grow
slowly to a dominating significance in this panorama,
and with that, to make more and more evident my
sense of the need of a creative assimilation, the cry
for synthetic effort, lest all this great being, this
splendid promise of a new world, should decay into
a vast unprogressive stagnation of unhappiness and
disorder. I have hinted at failures and cruelties, I
have put into the accumulating details of my vision,

children America blights, men she crushes, fine
hopes she disappoints and destroys. I have fcund
a place for the questioning figure of the South, the
sorrowful interrogation of the outcast colored people.
These are but the marginal shadows of a process in
its totality magnificent, but they exist, they go on
to mingle in her destinies.

Then I have tried to show, too, the conception I
have formed of the great skein of industrial competition that has been tightening and becoming
more and more involved through all this century-
long age, the age of blind growth, that draws now
towards its end; until the process threatens to
throttle individual freedom and individual enterprise altogether. And of a great mental uneasiness
and discontent, unprecedented in the history of the
American mind, that promises in the near future
some general and conscious endeavor to arrest this
unanticipated strangulation of freedom and free
living, some widespread struggle, of I know not what
constructive power, with the stains and disorders
and indignities that oppress and grow larger in the
national consciousness. I perceive more and more
that in coming to America I have chanced upon a
time of peculiar significance. The note of disillusionment sounds everywhere. America, for the
first time in her history, is taking thought about
herself, and ridding herself of long-cherished illusions.
I have already mentioned (in Chapter VIII.) the
memorable literature of self-examination that has

come into being during the last decade. Hitherto American thought has been extraordinarily localized; there has been no national press, in the sense that the press of London or Paris is national. Americans knew of America as a whole, mainly as the flag. Beneath the flag America is lost among constituent States and cities. All her newspapers have been, by English standards, "local" papers, preoccupied by local affairs, and taking an intensely localized point of view. A national newspaper for America would be altogether too immense an enterprise. Only since 1896, and in the form of weekly and monthly ten-cent magazines, have the rudiments of a national medium of expression appeared, and appeared to voice strange pregnant doubts. I had an interesting talk with Mr. Brisben Walker upon this new development. To him the first ten-cent magazine, *The Cosmopolitan*, was due, and he was naturally glad to tell me of the growth of this vehicle. To-day there is an aggregate circulation of ten millions of these magazines; they supply fiction, no doubt, and much of light interesting ephemeral matter, but not one of them is without its element of grave public discussion. I do not wish to make too much of this particular development, but regard it as a sign of new interests, of keen curiosities.

Now I must confess when I consider this ocean of readers I find the fears I have expressed of some analogical development of American affairs towards the stagnant commercialism of China, or towards a plutocratic imperialism and decadence of the Roman type, look singularly flimsy. Upon its present lines, and supposing there were no new sources of mental supply and energy, I do firmly believe that America might conceivably come more and more under the control of a tacitly organized and exhausting plutocracy, be swamped by a swelling tide of ignorant and unassimilable labor immigrants, decline towards violence and social misery, fall behind Europe in education and intelligence, and cease to lead civilization. In such a decay Cæsarism would be a most probable and natural phase, Cæsarism and a splitting into contending Cæsarisms. Come but a little sinking from intelligence towards coarseness and passion, and the South will yet endeavor to impose servitude anew upon its colored people, or secede—that trouble is not yet over. A little darkening and improverishment of outlook and New York would split from New England, and Colorado from the East. An illiterate, short-sighted America would be America doomed. But America is not illiterate; there are these great unprecedented reservoirs of intelligence and understanding, these millions of people who follow the process with an increasing comprehension. It is these millions of readers who make the American problem, and the problem of Europe and the world to-day, unique and incalculable, who provide a cohesive and reasonable and pacifying medium the Old World did not know.

THE MIND OF A MODERN STATE

II

You see, my hero in the confused Birth Struggles of a Common Mind drama of human life is intelligence; intelligence inspired by constructive passion. There is a demi-god imprisoned in mankind. All human history presents itself to me as the unconscious or half-unconscious struggle of human thought to emerge from the sightless interplay of instinct, individual passion, prejudice, and ignorance. One sees this diviner element groping after law and order and fine arrangement, like a thing blind and half-buried, in ancient Egypt, in ancient Judæa, in ancient Greece. It embodies its purpose in religions, invents the disciplines of morality, the reminders of ritual. It loses itself and becomes confused. It wearies and rests. In Plato, for the first time, one discovers it conscious and open-eyed, trying, indeed, to take hold of life and control it. Then it goes under, and becomes again a convulsive struggle, an inco-ordinated gripping and leaving, a muttering of literature and art, until the coming of our own times. Most painful and blundering of demi-gods it seems through all that space of years, with closed eyes and feverish effort. And now again it is clear to the minds of many men that they may lay hold upon and control the destiny of their kind. . . .

It is strange, it is often grotesque to mark how the reviving racial consciousness finds expression to-day. Now it startles itself into a new phase of self·

knowledge by striking a note from this art, and now by striking one from that. It breaks out in fiction that is ostensibly written only to amuse, it creeps into after-dinner discussions, and invades a press which is economically no more than a system of advertisement sheets proclaiming the price of the thing that is. Presently it is on the stage; the music-hall even is not safe from it. Youths walk in the streets to-day, talking together of things that were once the ultimate speculation of philosophy. I am no contemner of the present. To me it appears a time of immense and wonderful beginnings. New ideas are organizing themselves out of the little limited efforts of innumerable men. Never was there an age so intellectually prolific and abundant as this in the aggregate is. It is true, indeed, that we who write and think and investigate to-day, present nothing to compare with the magnificent reputations and intensely individualized achievements of the impressive personalities of the past. None the less is it true that taken all together we signifiy infinitely more. We no longer pose ourselves for admiration, high priests and princes of letters in a world of finite achievement; we admit ourselves no more than pages bearing the train of a Queen—but a Queen of limitless power. The knowledge we co-ordinate, the ideas we build together, the growing blaze in which we are willingly consumed, are wider and higher and richer in promise than anything the world has had before. . . .

THE MIND OF A MODERN STATE

When one takes count of the forces of intelligence upon which we may rely in the great conflict against matter, brute instinct, and individualistic disorder, to make the new social state, when we consider the organizing forms that emerge already from the general vague confusion, we find apparent in every modern state three chief series of developments. There is first the thinking and investigatory elements that grow constantly more important in our university life, the enlarging recognition of the need of a systematic issue of university publications, books, periodicals, and of sustained and fertilizing discussion. Then there is the greater, cruder, and bolder sea of mental activities outside academic limits, the amateurs, the free lances of thought and inquiry, the writers and artists, the innumerable ill-disciplined, untrained, but interested and well-meaning people who write and talk. They find their medium in contemporary literature, in journalism, in organizations for the propaganda of opinion. And, thirdly, there is the immense, nearly universally diffused system of education which, inadequately enough, serves to spread the new ideas as they are elaborated, which does, at any rate by its preparatory work, render them accessible. All these new manifestations of mind embody themselves in material forms, in class-rooms and laboratories, in libraries, and a vast machinery of book and newspaper production and distribution.

Consider the new universities that spring up all over America. Almost imperceptibly throughout the past century, little by little, the conception of a university has changed, until now it is nearly altogether changed. The old-time university was a collection of learned men; it believed that all the generalizations had been made, all the fundamental things said; it had no vistas towards the future; it existed for teaching and exercises, and more than half implied what Dr. Johnson, for example, believed, that secular degeneration was the rule of human life. All that, you know, has gone; every university, even Oxford (though, poor pretentious dear, she still professes to read and think metaphysics in "the original" Greek) admits the conception of a philosophy that progresses, that broadens and intensifies, age by age. But to come to America is to come to a country far more alive to the thinking and knowledge-making function of universities than Great Britain. One splendidly endowed foundation, the Johns Hopkins University, Baltimore, exists only for research, and that was the first intention of Chicago University also. In sociology, in pedagogics, in social psychology, these vital sciences for the modern state, America is producing an amount of work which, however trivial in proportion to the task before her, is at any rate immense in comparison with our own British output. . . .

THE MIND OF A MODERN STATE

III

Columbia University I DID my amateurish and transitory best to see something of the American universities. There was Columbia. Thither I went with a letter to Professor Giddings, whose sociological writings are world famous. I found him busy with a secretary in a business-like little room, stowed away somewhere under the dome of the magnificent building of the university library. He took me round the opulent spaces, the fine buildings of Columbia. . . . I suppose it is inevitable that a visitor should see the constituents of a university out of proportion, but I came away with an impression overwhelmingly architectural. The library dome, I confess, was fine, and the desks below well filled with students, the books were abundant, well arranged, and well tended. But I recall marble staircases, I recall great wastes of marble steps, I recall, in particular, students' baths of extraordinary splendor, and I do not recall anything like an equivalent effect of large leisure and dignity for intellectual men. Professor Giddings seemed driven and busy, the few men I met there appeared all to have a lot of immediate work to do. It occurred to me in Columbia, as it occurred to me later in the University of Chicago, that the disposition of the university founder is altogether too much towards buildings and memorial inscriptions, and all too little towards the more difficult and far more valuable end of putting

men of pre-eminent ability into positions of stimulat-
ed leisure. This is not a distinctly American effect.
In Oxford, just as much as in Columbia, nay, far
more! you find stone and student lording it over the
creative mental thing; the dons go about like some
sort of little short-coated parasite, pointing respect-
fully to tower and façade, which have, in truth, no
reason for existing except to shelter them. Columbia
is almost as badly off for means of publication as
Oxford, and quite as poor in inducements towards
creative work. Professors talk in an altogether
British way of getting work done in the vaca-
tion.

Moreover, there was an effect of remoteness about
Columbia. It may have been the quality of a blue
still morning of sunshine that invaded my impression. I came up out of the crowded tumult of New
York to it, with a sense of the hooting, hurrying
traffics of the wide harbor, the teeming East Side,
the glitter of spending, the rush of finance, the whole
headlong process of America, behind me. I came
out of the subway station into wide still streets. It
was very spacious, very dignified, very quiet. Well,
I want the universities of the modern state to be
more aggressive. I want to think of a Columbia
University of a less detached appearance, even if she
is less splendidly clad. I want to think of her as
sitting up there, cheek on hand, with knitted brows,
brooding upon the millions below. I want to think
of all the best minds conceivable going to and fro—

thoughts and purposes in her organized mind. And when she speaks that busy world should listen. . . .

As a matter of fact, much of that busy world still regards a professor as something between a dealer in scientific magic and a crank, and a university as an institution every good American should be honestly proud of and avoid.

IV

HARVARD, too, is detached, though not quite with the same immediacy of contrast. Harvard reminded me very much of my first impressions of Oxford. One was taken about in the same way to see this or that point of view. Much of Harvard is Georgian red brick, that must have seemed very ripe and venerable until a year or so ago one bitter winter killed all the English ivy. There are students' clubs, after the fashion of the Oxford Union, but finer and better equipped; there is an amazing Germanic museum, the gift of the present Emperor, that does, in a con-centrated form, present all that is flamboyant of Germany; there are noble museums and libraries, and very many fine and dignified aspects and spaces, and an abundant intellectual life. Harvard is hap-pily free from the collegiate politics that absorb most of the surplus mental energy of Oxford and Cambridge, and the professors can and do meet and talk. At Harvard men count. I was condoled with

Harvard

213

on all hands in my disappointment that I could not meet Professor William James—he was still in California—and I had the good fortune to meet and talk to President Eliot, who is, indeed, a very considerable voice in American affairs. To me he talked quite readily and frankly of a very living subject, the integrity of the press in relation to the systematic and successful efforts of the advertising chemists and druggists to stifle exposures of noxious proprietary articles. He saw the problem as the subtle play of group psychology it is; there was none of that feeble horror of these troubles as "modern and vulgar" that one would expect in an English university leader. I fell into a great respect for his lean fine face and figure, his deliberate voice, his open, balanced, and constructive mind. He was the first man I had met who had any suggestion of a force and quality that might stand up to and prevail against the forces of acquisition and brute trading. He bore himself as though some sure power were behind him, unlike many other men I met who criticised abuses abusively, or in the key of facetious despair. He had very much of that fine aristocratic quality one finds cropping up so frequently among Americans of old tradition, an aristocratic quality that is free from either privilege or pretension. . . .

At Harvard, too, I met Professor Münsterberg, one of the few writers of standing who have attempted a general review of the American situation. He is a tall fair German, but newly annexed to America, with a certain diplomatic quality in his personality, standing almost consciously, as it were, for Germany in America, and for America in Germany. He has written a book for either people, because hitherto they have seen each other too much through English media ("von Englischen linseln retouchiert"), and he has done much to spread the conception of a common quality and sympathy between Germany and America. "Blood," he says in this connection, "is thicker than water, but . . . printer's ink is thicker than blood." England is too aristocratic, France too shockingly immoral, Russia too absolutist to be the sympathetic and similar friend of America, and so, by a process of exhaustion, Germany remains the one power on earth capable of an "inner understanding." (Also he has drawn an alluring parallel between President Roosevelt and the Emperor William to complete the approximation of "die beiden Edelnationen"). I had read all this, and was interested to encounter him therefore at a Harvard table in a circle of his colleagues, agreeable and courteous, and still scarcely more assimilated than the brightly new white Germanic museum among the red brick traditions of Kirkland and Cambridge streets. . . .

Harvard impresses me altogether as a very living factor in the present American outlook, not only when I was in Cambridge, but in the way the place *tells* in New York, in Chicago, in Washington. It has a living and contemporary attitude, and it is

THE FUTURE IN AMERICA

becoming more and more audible. Harvard opinion
influences the magazines and affects the press, at
least in the East, to an increasing extent. It may,
in the near future, become still more rapidly audible.
Professor Eliot is now full of years and honor, and I
found in New York, in Boston, in Washington, that
his successor was being discussed. In all these
cities I met people disposed to believe that if President Roosevelt does not become President of the
United States for a further term, he may succeed
President Eliot. Now that I have seen President
Roosevelt it seems to me that this might have a most
extraordinary effect in accelerating the reaction
upon the people of America of the best and least
mercenary of their national thought. Already he is
exerting an immense influence in the advertisement
of new ideas and ideals. But of President Roosevelt
I shall write more fully later. . . .

V

CHICAGO UNIVERSITY, too, is a splen-
Chicago Uni-
versity did place of fine buildings and green
spaces and trees, with a great going to
and fro of students, a wonderful contrast to the dark
congestions of the mercantile city to the north. To
all the disorganization of that it is even physically
antagonistic, and I could think as I went about it
that already this new organization has produced such

A BIT OF PRINCETON UNIVERSITY

writing as Veblen's admirable ironies (*The Theory of Business Enterprise*, for example), and such sociological work as that of Zueblin and Albion Small. I went through the vigorous and admirably equipped pedagogic department, which is evidently a centre of thought and stimulus for the whole teaching profession of Illinois; I saw a library of sociology and economics beyond anything that London can boast; I came upon little groups of students working amid piles of books in a businesslike manner, and if at times in other sections this suggestion was still insistent that thought was as yet only "moving in" and, as it were, getting the carpets down, it was equally clear that thought was going to live freely and spaciously, to an unprecedented extent, so soon as things were in order.

I visited only these three great foundations, each in its materially embodiment already larger, wealthier, and more hopeful than any contemporary British institution, and it required an effort to realize that they were but a portion of the embattled universities of America, that I had not seen Yale nor Princeton nor Cornell nor Leland Stanford nor any Western State university, not a tithe, indeed, of America's drilling levies in the coming war of thought against chaos. I am in no way equipped to estimate the value of the drilling; I have been unable to get any conception how far these tens of thousands of students in these institutions are really *alive* intellectually, are really inquiring, discussing, reading,

and criticising; I have no doubt the great numbers of
them spend many hours after the fashion of one
roomful I saw intent upon a blackboard covered
with Greek; but allowing the utmost for indolence,
games, distractions, and waste of time and energy
upon unfruitful and obsolete studies, the fact of this
great increasing proportion of minds at least a little
trained in things immaterial, a little exercised in the
critical habit, remains a fact to put over against that
million and a half child workers who can barely have
learned to read—the other side, the redeeming side
of the American prospect.

VI

A Voice from Cornell I AM impressed by the evident consciousness of the American universities
of the rôle they have to play in America's future. They seem to me pervaded by the
constructive spirit. They are intelligently antagonistic to lethargic and self-indulgent traditions, to
disorder, and disorderly institutions. It is from the
universities that the deliberate invasion of the
political machine by independent men of honor and
position—of whom President Roosevelt is the type
and chief—proceeds. Mr. George Iles has called
my attention to a remarkable address made so long
ago as the year 1883 before the Yale Alumni, by
President Andrew D. White (the first president), of

Cornell, who was afterwards American Ambassador at St. Petersburg and Berlin. President White was a member of the class of '53, and he addressed himself particularly to the men of that year. His title was "The Message of the Nineteenth Century to the Twentieth," and it is full of a spirit that grows and spreads throughout American life, that may ultimately spread throughout the life of the whole nation, a spirit of criticism and constructive effort, of a scope and quality the world has never seen before. The new class of '83 are the messengers.

"To a few tottering old men of our dear class of '53 it will be granted to look with straining eyes over the boundary into the twentieth century; but even these can do little to make themselves heard then. Most of us shall not see it. But before us and around us; nay, in our own families are the men who shall see it. The men who go forth from these dear shades to-morrow are girding themselves for it. Often as I have stood in the presence of such bands of youthful messengers I have never been able to resist a feeling of awe, as in my boyhood when I stood before men who were soon to see Palestine and the Far East, or the Golden Gates of the West, and the islands of the Pacific. The old story of St. Fillipo Neri at Rome comes back to me, who, in the days of the Elizabethan persecutions, made men bring him out into the open air and set him opposite the door of the Papal College of Rome, that he might look into the faces of the English students, destined to go forth to triumph or to martyrdom for the faith in far-off, heretic England."

I cannot forbear from quoting further from this address; it is all so congenial to my own beliefs. Indeed, I like to think of that gathering of young men and old as if it were still existing, as though the old fellows of '53 were still sitting listening and looking up responsive to this appeal that comes down to us. I fancy President White on the platform before them, a little figure in the perspective of a quarter of a century, but still quite clearly audible, delivering his periods to that now indistinguishable audience:

"What, then, is to be done? Mercantilism, necessitated at first by our circumstances and position, has been in the main a great blessing. It has been so under a simple law of history. How shall it be prevented from becoming in obedience to a similar inexorable law, a curse?

"Here, in the answer to this question, it seems to me, is the most important message from this century to the next.

"For the great thing to be done is neither more nor less than to develop *other* great elements of civilization now held in check, which shall take their rightful place in the United States, which shall modify the mercantile spirit, . . . which shall make the history of our country something greater and broader than anything we have reached, or ever can reach, under the sway of mercantilism alone.

"What shall be those counter elements of civilization? Monarchy, aristocracy, militarism we could not have if we would, we would not have if we could. What shall we have?

"I answer simply that we must do all that we can to rear greater fabrics of religious, philosophic thought, literary thought, scientific, artistic, political thought to summon young men more and more into these fields, not as a matter of taste or social opportunity, but as a patriotic duty; to hold before them not the incentive of mere gain or of mere pleasure or of mere reputation, but the ideal of a new and higher civilization. The greatest work which the coming century has to do in this country is to build up an aristocracy of thought and feeling which shall hold its own against the aristocracy of mercantilism. I would have more and more the appeal made to every young man who feels within him the ability to do good or great things in any of these higher fields, to devote his powers to them as a sacred duty, no matter how strongly the mercantile or business spirit may draw him. I would have the idea preached early and late. . . .

"And as the guardian of such a movement, . . . I would strengthen at every point this venerable university, and others like it throughout the country. Remiss, indeed, have the graduates and friends of our own honored Yale been in their treatment of her. She has never had the means to do a tithe of what she might do. She ought to be made strong enough, with more departments, more professors, more fellowships, to become one of a series of great rallying points or fortresses, and to hold always concentrated here a strong army, ever active against mercantilism, materialism, and Philistinism. . . .

"But, after all, the effort to create these new counterpoising, modifying elements of a greater civilization must be begun in the individual man, and especially in the youth who feels within himself the power to think, the power to write, the power to carve the marble, to paint, to leave something behind him better than dollars. In the individual minds and hearts and souls of the messengers who are preparing for the next century is a source of regeneration. They must form an ideal of religion higher than that of a life devoted to grasping and grinding and griping, with a whine for mercy at the end of it. They must form an ideal of science higher than that of increasing the production of iron or cotton. They must form an ideal of literature and of art higher than that of pandering to the latest prejudice or whimsey. And they must form an ideal of man himself worthy of that century into which are to be poured the accumulations of this. So shall material elements be brought to their proper place, made stronger for good, made harmless for evil. So shall we have that development of new and greater elements, that balance of principles which shall make this republic greater than anything of which we now can dream."

CHAPTER XIV

CULTURE

I

The Boston
Enchantment

YET even as I write of the universities as the central intellectual organ of a modern state, as I sit implying salvation by schools, there comes into my mind a mass of qualification. The devil in the American world drama may be mercantilism, ensnaring, tempting, battling against my hero, the creative mind of man, but mercantilism is not the only antagonist. In Fifth Avenue or Paterson one may find nothing but the zenith and nadir of the dollar hunt, at a Harvard table one may encounter nothing but living minds, but in Boston—I mean not only Beacon Street and Commonwealth Avenue, but that Boston of the mind and heart that pervades American refinement and goes about the world—one finds the human mind not base, nor brutal, nor stupid, nor ignorant, but mysteriously enchanting and ineffectual, so that having eyes it yet does not see, having powers it achieves nothing. . . .

I remember Boston as a quiet effect, as something a little withdrawn, as a place standing aside from the

throbbing interchange of East and West. When I
hear the word Boston now it is that quality returns.
I do not think of the spreading parkways of Mr.
Woodbury and Mr. Olmstead nor of the crowded
harbor; the congested tenement-house regions, full
of those aliens whose tongues struck so strangely on
the ears of Mr. Henry James, come not to mind.
But I think of rows of well-built, brown and ruddy
homes, each with a certain sound architectural
distinction, each with its two squares of neatly
trimmed grass between itself and the broad, quiet
street, and each with its family of cultured people
within. I am reminded of deferential but un-
ostentatious servants, and of being ushered into
large, dignified entrance-halls. I think of spacious
stairways, curtained archways, and rooms of agreeable, receptive persons. I recall the finished in-
formality of the high tea. All the people of my impression have been taught to speak English with a
quite admirable intonation; some of the men and
most of the women are proficient in two or three
languages; they have travelled in Italy, they have
all the recognized classics of European literature in
their minds, and apt quotations at command. And
I think of the constant presence of treasured associations with the titanic and now mellowing literary reputations of Victorian times, with Emerson
(who called Poe "that jingle man"), and with Longfellow, whose house is now sacred, its view towards
the Charles River and the stadium—it is a real,

correct stadium — secured by the purchase of the sward before it forever. . . .

At the mention of Boston I think, too, of autotypes and then of plaster casts. I do not think I shall ever see an autotype again without thinking of Boston. I think of autotypes of the supreme masterpieces of sculpture and painting, and particularly of the fluttering garments of the "Nike of Samothrace." (That I saw, also, in little casts and big, and photographed from every conceivable point of view.) It is incredible how many people in Boston have selected her for their æsthetic symbol and expression. Always that lady was in evidence about me, unobtrusively persistent, until at last her frozen stride pursued me into my dreams. That frozen stride became the visible spirit of Boston in my imagination, a sort of blind, headless, and unprogressive fine resolution that took no heed of any contemporary thing. Next to that I recall, as inseparably Bostonian, the dreaming grace of Botticelli's "Prima vera." All Bostonians admire Botticelli, and have a feeling for the roof of the Sistine chapel—to so casual and adventurous a person as myself, indeed, Boston presents a terrible, a terrifying unanimity of æsthetic discriminations. I was nearly brought back to my childhood's persuasion that, after all, there is a right and wrong in these things. And Boston clearly thought the less of Mr. Bernard Shaw when I told her he had induced me to buy a pianola, not that Boston ever did set much store by so contemporary a person as Mr. Bernard Shaw. The books she reads are toned and seasoned books—preferably in the old or else in limited editions, and by authors who may be lectured upon without decorum. . . .

Boston has in her symphony concerts the best music in America, and here her tastes are severely orthodox and classic. I heard Beethoven's Fifth Symphony extraordinarilv well done, the familiar pinnacled Fifth Symphony, and now, whenever I grind that out upon the convenient mechanism beside my desk at home, mentally I shall be transferred to Boston again, shall hear its magnificent aggressive thumpings transfigured into exquisite orchestration, and sit again among that audience of pleased and pleasant ladies in chaste, high-necked, expensive dresses, and refined, attentive, appreciative, bald, or iron-gray men. . . .

II

Then Boston has historical associa-
Boston's Antiquity
tions that impressed me like iron-moulded, leather-bound, eighteenth-century books. The War of Independence, that to us in England seems half-way back to the days of Elizabeth, is a thing of yesterday in Boston. "Here," your host will say and pause, "came marching" so-and-so, "with his troops to relieve" so-and-so. And you will find he is the great-grandson of so-and-so. and still keeps that ancient colonial's sword. And

226

these things happened before they dug the Hythe military canal, before Sandgate, except for a decrepit castle, existed; before the days when Bonaparte gathered his army at Boulogne—in the days of muskets and pigtails—and erected that column my telescope at home can reach for me on a clear day. All that is ancient history in England and in Boston the decade before those distant alarums and excursions is yesterday. A year or so ago they restored the British arms to the old State-House. "Feeling," my informant witnessed, "was dying down." But there were protests, nevertheless. . . .

If there is one note of incongruity in Boston, it is in the gilt dome of the Massachusetts State-House at night. They illuminate it with electric light. That shocked me as an anachronism. It shocked me—much as it would have shocked me to see one of the colonial portraits, or even one of the endless autotypes of the Belvidere Apollo replaced, let us say, by one of Mr. Alvin Coburn's wonderfully beautiful photographs of modern New York. That electric glitter breaks the spell; it is the admission of the present, of the twentieth century. It is just as if the Quirinal and Vatican took to an exchange of badinage with search-lights, or the King mounted an illuminated E. R. on the Round Tower at Windsor.

Save for that one discord there broods over the real Boston an immense effect of finality. One feels in Boston, as one feels in no other part of the States, that the intellectual movement has ceased.

Boston is now producing no literature except a
little criticism. Contemporary Boston art is imitative art, its writers are correct and imitative writers
the central figure of its literary world is that charming old lady of eighty-eight, Mrs. Julia Ward Howe.
One meets her and Colonel Higginson in the midst of
an authors' society that is not so much composed of
minor stars as a chorus of indistinguishable culture.
There are an admirable library and a museum in
Boston, and the library is Italianate, and decorated
within like an ancient missal. In the less ornamental
spaces of this place there are books and readers.
There is particularly a charming large room for
children, full of pigmy chairs and tables, in which
quite little tots sit reading. I regret now I did not
ascertain precisely what they were reading, but I
have no doubt it was classical matter.

I do not know why the full sensing of what is ripe
and good in the past should carry with it this quality
of discriminating against the present and the future.
The fact remains that it does so almost oppressively.
I found myself by some accident of hospitality one
evening in the company of a number of Boston
gentlemen who constituted a book-collecting club.
They had dined, and they were listening to a paper
on Bibles printed in America. It was a scholarly,
valuable, and exhaustive piece of research. The sur-
viving copies of each edition were traced, and when
some rare specimen was mentioned as the property
of any member of the club there was decorously

warm applause. I had been seeing Boston, drinking in the Boston atmosphere all day. . . . I know it will seem an ungracious and ungrateful thing to confess (yet the necessities of my picture of America compel me), but as I sat at the large and beautifully ordered table, with these fine, rich men about me, and listened to the steady progress of the reader's ever unrhetorical sentences, and the little bursts of approval, it came to me with a horrible quality of conviction that the mind of the world was dead, and that this was a distribution of souvenirs.

Indeed, so strongly did this grip me that presently, upon some slight occasion, I excused myself and went out into the night. I wandered about Boston for some hours, trying to shake off this unfortunate idea. I felt that all the books had been written, all the pictures painted, all the thoughts said—or at least that nobody would ever believe this wasn't so. I felt it was dreadful nonsense to go on writing books. Nothing remained but to collect them in the richest, finest manner one could. Somewhere about midnight I came to a publisher's window, and stood in the dim moonlight peering enviously at piled copies of Izaak Walton and Omar Khayyam, and all the happy immortals who got in before the gates were shut. And then in the corner I discovered a thin, small book. For a time I could scarcely believe my eyes. I lit a match to be the surer. And it was *A Modern Symposium*, by Lowes Dickinson, beyond all disputing. It was strangely comforting to see it there—a leaf of olive from the world of thought I had imagined drowned forever.

That was just one night's mood. I do not wish to accuse Boston of any wilful, deliberate repudiation of the present and the future. But I think that Boston—when I say Boston let the reader always understand I mean that intellectual and spiritual Boston that goes about the world, that traffics in book-shops in Rome and Piccadilly, that I have dined with and wrangled with in my friend W.'s house in Blackheath, dear W., who, I believe, has never seen America—I think, I say, that Boston commits the scholastic error and tries to remember too much, to treasure too much, and has refined and studied and collected herself into a state of hopeless intellectual and æsthetic repletion in consequence. In these matters there are limits. The finality of Boston is a quantitive consequence. The capacity of Boston, it would seem, was just sufficient but no more than sufficient, to comprehend the whole achievement of the human intellect up, let us say, to the year 1875 A.D. Then an equilibrium was established. At or about that year Boston filled up.

III

IT is the peculiarity of Boston's in-
About Wellesley tellectual quality that she cannot unload again. She treasures Longfellow in quantity. She treasures his works, she treasures

associations, she treasures his Cambridge home.
Now, really, to be perfectly frank about him, Longfellow is not good enough for that amount of intellectual house room. He cumbers Boston. And
when I went out to Wellesley to see that delightful
girls' college everybody told me I should be reminded of the "Princess." For the life of me I
could not remember what "Princess." Much of my
time in Boston was darkened by the constant strain
of concealing the frightful gaps in my intellectual
baggage, this absence of things I might reasonably
be supposed, as a cultivated person, to have, but
which, as a matter of fact, I'd either left behind,
never possessed, or deliberately thrown away. I
felt instinctively that Boston could never possibly
understand the light travelling of a philosophical
carpet-bagger. But I hid—in full view of the tree-
set Wellseley lake, ay, with the skiffs of "sweet girl
graduates"—own up. "I say," I said, "I wish
you wouldn't all be so allusive. *What* Princess?"

It was, of course, that thing of Tennyson's. It is
a long, frequently happy and elegant, and always
meritorious narrative poem, in which a chaste Victorian amorousness struggles with the early formulæ
of the feminist movement. I had read it when I
was a boy, I was delighted to be able to claim,
and had honorably forgotten the incident. But in
Boston they treat it as a living classic, and expect
you to remember constantly and with appreciation
this passage and that. I think that quite typical

of the Bostonian weakness. It is the error of the clever high-school girl, it is the mistake of the scholastic mind all the world over, to learn too thoroughly and to carry too much. They want to know and remember Longfellow and Tennyson— just as in art they want to know and remember Raphael and all the elegant inanity of the sacrifice at Lystra, or the miraculous draught of Fishes; just as in history they keep all the picturesque legends of the War of Independence—looking up the dates and minor names, one imagines, ever and again. Some years ago I met two Boston ladies in Rome. Each day they sallied forth from our hotel to see and appreciate; each evening, after dinner, they revised and underlined in Baedeker what they had seen. *They meant to miss nothing in Rome.* It's fine in its way—this receptive eagerness, this learners' avidity. Only people who can go about in this spirit need, if their minds are to remain mobile, not so much heads as *cephalic pantechnicon vans.* . . .

IV

The Wellesley
Cabinets I FIND this appetite to have all the mellow and refined and beautiful things in life to the exclusion of all thought for the present and the future even in the sweet, free air of Wellesley's broad park, that most delightful, that almost incredible girls' university, with its class - rooms, its halls of residence, its club - houses and gathering-places among the glades and trees. I have very vivid in my mind a sunlit room in which girls were copying the detail in the photographs of masterpieces, and all around this room were cabinets of drawers, and in each drawer photographs. There must be in that room photographs of every picture of the slightest importance in Italy, and detailed studies of many. I suppose, too, there are photographs of all the sculpture and buildings in Italy that are by any standard considerable. There is, indeed, a great civilization, stretching over centuries and embodying the thought and devotion, the scepticism and levities, the ambition, the pretensions, the passions, and desires of innumerable sinful and world-used men—*canned*, as it were, in this one room, and freed from any deleterious ingredients. The young ladies, under the direction of competent instructors, go through it, no doubt, industriously, and emerge—capable of Browning.

I was taken into two or three charming club-houses that dot this beautiful domain. There was a Shakespeare club-house, with a delightful theatre, Elizabethan in style, and all set about with Shakespearean things; there was the club-house of the girls who are fitting themselves for their share in the great American problem by the study of Greek. Groups of pleasant girls in each, grave with the fine gravity of youth, entertained the reluctantly critical visitor, and were unmistakably delighted and relaxed when one made it clear that one was not in the Great Teacher line of business, when one confided that one was there on false pretences, and insisting on seeing the pantry. They have jolly little pantries, and they make excellent tea.

I returned to Boston at last in a state of mighty doubting, provided with a Wellesley College calendar to study at my leisure.

I cannot, for the life of me, determine how far Wellesley is an aspect of what I have called Boston; how far it is a part of that wide forward movement of the universities upon which I lavish hope and blessings. Those drawings of photographed Madonnas and Holy Families and Annunciations, the sustained study of Greek, the class in the French drama of the seventeenth century, the study of the topography of Rome fill me with misgivings, seeing the world is in torment for the want of living thought about its present affairs. But, on the other hand, there are courses upon socialism—though the textbook is still *Das Kapital* of Marx—and upon the industrial history of England and America. I didn't discover a debating society, but there is a large accessible library.

How far, I wonder still, are these girls thinking and feeding mentally for themselves? What do they discuss one with another? How far do they suffer under that plight of feminine education—notetaking from lectures? . . .

But, after all, this about Wellesley is a digression

234

into which I fell by way of Boston's autotypes. My main thesis was that culture, as it is conceived in Boston, is no contribution to the future of America, that cultivated people may be, in effect, as state-blind as—Mr. Morgan Richards. It matters little in the mind of the world whether any one is concentrated upon mediæval poetry, Florentine pictures, or the propagation of pills. The common, significant fact in all these cases is this, a blindness to the crude splendor of the possibilities of America now, to the tragic greatness of the unheeded issues that blunder towards solution. Frankly, I grieve over Boston—Boston throughout the world—as a great waste of leisure and energy, as a frittering away of moral and intellectual possibilities. We give too much to the past. New York is not simply more interesting than Rome, but more significant, more stimulating, and far more beautiful, and the idea that to be concerned about the latter in preference to the former is a mark of a finer mental quality is one of the most mischievous and foolish ideas that ever invaded the mind of man. We are obsessed by the scholastic prestige of mere knowledge and genteel remoteness. Over against unthinking ignorance is scholarly refinement, the spirit of Boston; between that Scylla and this Charybdis the creative mind of man steers its precarious way.

CHAPTER XV

AT WASHINGTON

I

I CAME to Washington full of expectations and curiosities. Here, I felt, so
far as it could exist visibly and palpably
anywhere, was the head and mind of this colossal
America over which my observant curiosities had
wandered. In this place I should find, among other
things, perhaps as many as ten thousand men who
would not be concerned in trade. There would be
all the Senators and representatives, their secre-
taries and officials, and four thousand and more
scientific and literary men of Washington's institutions and libraries, the diplomatic corps, the educational centres, the civil service, the writers and
thinking men who must inevitably be drawn to this
predestined centre. I promised myself arduous intercourse with a teeming intellectual life. Here I
should find questions answered, discover missing
clues, get hold of the last connections in my inquiry.
I should complete at Washington my vision of
America; my forecast would follow.

I don't precisely remember how this vision departed. I know only that after a day or so in Washington an entirely different conception was established, a conception of Washington as architecture and avenues, as a place of picture post-cards and excursions, with sightseers instead of thoughts going to and fro. I had imagined that in Washington I should find such mentally vigorous discussion-centres as the New York X Club on a quite magnificent scale. Instead, I found the chief scientific gathering-place has, like so many messes in the British army before the Boer war, a rule against talking "shop." In all Washington there is no clearing-house of thought at all; Washington has no literary journals, no magazines, no publications other than those of the official specialist—there does not seem to be a living for a single firm of publishers in this magnificent empty city.

I went about the place in a state of ridiculous and deepening concern. I went though the splendid Botanical Gardens, through the spacious and beautiful Capitol, and so to the magnificently equipped Library of Congress. There in an upper chamber that commands an altogether beautiful view of long vistas of avenue and garden to that stupendous unmeaning obelisk (the work of the women of America) that dominates all Washington, I found at last a little group of men who could talk. It was like a small raft upon a limitless empty sea. I lunched with them at their Round Table, and afterwards Mr.

Putnam showed me the Rotunda, quite the most gracious reading-room dome the world possesses, and explained the wonderful mechanical organization that brings almost every volume in that immense collection within a minute of one's hand. "With all this," I asked him, "why doesn't the place *think?*" He seemed, discreetly, to consider it did.

It was in the vein of Washington's detached deadness that I should find Professor Langley (whose flying experiments I have followed for some years with close interest) was dead, and I went through the long galleries of archæological specimens and stuffed animals in the Smithsonian Institution to inflict my questions upon his temporary successor, Dr. Cyrus Adler. He had no adequate excuses. He found a kind of explanation in the want of enterprise of American publishers, so that none of them come to Washington to tap its latent resources of knowledge and intellectual capacity; but that does not account for the absence of any traffic in ideas. It is perhaps near the truth to say that this dearth of any general and comprehensive intellectual activity is due to intellectual specialization. The four thousand scientific men in Washington are all too energetically busy with ethnographic details, electrical computations, or herbaria to talk about common and universal things. They ought not to be so busy, and a science so specialized sinks half-way down the scale of sciences. Science is one of those things that cannot hustle; if it does, it loses its con-

IN THE CONGRESSIONAL LIBRARY

nections. In Washington some men, I gathered, hustle, others play bridge, and general questions are left, a little contemptuously, as being of the nature of "gas," to the newspapers and magazines. Philosophy, which correlates the sciences and keeps them subservient to the universals of life, has no seat there. My anticipated synthesis of ten thousand minds refused, under examination, to synthesize at all; it remained disintegrated, a mob, individually active and collectively futile, of specialists and politicians.

II

BUT that is only one side of Washington life, the side east and south of the White House. Northwestward I found, I confess, the most agreeable social atmosphere in America. It is a region of large fine houses, of dignified and ample-minded people, people not given over to "smartness" nor redolent of dollars, unhurried and reflective, not altogether lost to the wider aspects of life. In Washington I met again that peculiarly aristocratic quality I had found in Harvard—in the person of President Eliot, for example—an aristocratic quality that is all the finer for the absence of rank, that has integral in it—books, thought, and responsibility. And yet I could have wished these fine people more alive to

The City of Conversation

present and future things, a little less established upon completed and mellowing foundations, a little less final in their admirable finish. . . .

There was, I found, a little breeze of satisfaction fluttering the Washington atmosphere in this region. Mr. Henry James came through the States last year distributing epithets among their cities with the justest aptitude. Washington was the "City of Conversation"; and she was pleasantly conscious that she merited this friendly coronation.

Washington, indeed, converses well, without awkwardness, without chatterings, kindly, watchful, agreeably witty. She lulled and tamed my purpose to ask about primary things, to discuss large questions. Only once, and that was in an after-dinner duologue, did I get at all into a question in Washington. For the rest, Washington remarked and alluded and made her point and got away.

III

AND Washington, with a remarkable Mount Vernon unanimity and in the most charming manner, assured me that if I came to see and understand America I must on no account miss Mount Vernon. To have passed indifferently by Concord was bad enough, I was told, but to ignore the home of the first president, to turn my back upon that ripe monument of colonial simplicity, would be quite criminal neglect. To me it was a revelation how sincerely insistent they were upon this. It reminded me of an effect I had already appreciated very keenly in Boston—and even before Boston, when Mr. Z took me across Spuyten Duyvil into the country of Sleepy Hollow, and spoke of Cornwallis as though he had died yesterday—and that is the longer historical perspectives of America. America is an older country than any European one, for she has not rejuvenesced for a hundred and thirty years. In endless ways America fails to be contemporary. In many respects, no doubt, she is decades in front of Europe, in mechanism, for example, and productive organization, but in very many other and more fundamental ones she is decades behind. Go but a little way back and you will find the European's perspectives close up; they close at '71, at '48, down a vista of reform bills, at Waterloo and the treaty of Paris, at the Irish Union, at the coming of Victor Emanuel; Great Britain, for example, in the last hundred years has reconstructed politically and socially, created half her present peerage, evolved the Empire of India, developed Australia, New Zealand, South Africa, fought fifty considerable wars. Mount Vernon, on the other hand, goes back with unbroken continuity, a broad band of mellow tradition, to the War of Independence.

Well, I got all that in conversation at Washington, and so I didn't need to go to Mount Vernon, after all. I got all that about 1777, and I failed altogether to get anything of any value whatever about 1977—which is the year of greater interest to me. About the direction and destinies of that great American process that echoes so remotely through Washington's cool gracefulness of architecture and her umbrageous parks, this cultivated society seemed to me to be terribly incurious and indifferent. It was alive to political personalities, no doubt, its sons and husbands were Senators, judges, ambassadors, and the like; it was concerned with their speeches and prospects, but as to the trend of the whole thing Washington does not picture it, does not want to picture it. I found myself presently excusing myself for Mount Vernon on the ground that I was not a retrospective American, but a go-ahead Englishman, and so apologizing for my want of reverence for venerable things. "We are a young people," I maintained. "We are a new generation."

IV

I WENT to see the Senate debating the
In the Senate-House railway-rate bill, and from the Senatorial gallery I had pointed out to me Tillman and Platt, Foraker and Lodge, and all the varied personalities of the assembly. The chamber is a circular one, with enormously capacious galleries. The members speak from their desks, other members write letters, read (and rustle) newspapers, sit

among accumulations of torn paper, or stand round the apartment in audibly conversational groups. A number of messenger-boys—they wear no uniform —share the floor of the House with the representatives, and are called by clapping the hands. They go to and fro, or sit at the feet of the Vice-President. Behind and above the Vice-President the newspaper men sit in a state of partial attention, occasionally making notes for the vivid descriptions that have long since superseded verbatim reports in America. The public galleries contain hundreds of intermittently talkative spectators. For the most part these did not seem to me to represent, as the little strangers' gallery in the House of Commons represents, interests affected. They were rather spectators seeing Washington, taking the Senate *en route* for the obelisk top and Mount Vernon. They made little attempt to hear the speeches.

In a large distinguished emptiness among these galleries is the space devoted to diplomatic representatives, and there I saw, sitting in a meritorious solitude, the British *charge d'affaires* and his wife following the debate below. I found it altogether too submerged for me to follow. The countless spectators, the Senators, the boy messengers, the comings and goings kept up a perpetual confusing babblement. One saw men walking carelessly between the Speaker and the Vice-President, and at one time two gentlemen with their backs to the member in possession of the House engaged the Vice-President in an earnest conversation. The messengers circulated at a brisk trot, or sat on the edge of the dais exchanging subdued badinage. I have never seen a more distracted Legislature.

The whole effect of Washington is a want of concentration, of something unprehensile and apart. It is on, not in, the American process. The place seems to me to reflect, even in its sounds and physical forms, that dispersal of power, that evasion of a simple conclusiveness, which is the peculiar effect of that ancient compromise, the American Constitution. The framers of that treaty were haunted by two terrible bogies, a military dictatorship and what they called "mob rule," they were obsessed by the need of safeguards against these dangers, they were controlled by the mutual distrust of constituent States far more alien to one another than they are now, and they failed to foresee both the enormous assimilation of interests and character presently to be wrought by the railways and telegraphs, and the huge possibilities of corruption, elaborate electrical arrangements offer to clever unscrupulous men. And here in Washington is the result, a Legislature that fails to legislate, a government that cannot govern, a pseudo-responsible administration that offers enormous scope for corruption, and that is perhaps invincibly intrenched behind the two-party system from any insurgence of the popular will. The plain fact of the case is that Congress, as it is constituted at present, is the feeblest, least accessible, and most inefficient central government of any civilized nation in the worst west of Russia. Congress is entirely inadequate to the tasks of the present time.

I came away from Washington with my preconception enormously reinforced that the supreme need of America, the preliminary thing to any social or economic reconstruction, is political reform. It seems to me to lie upon the surface that America has to be democratized. It is necessary to make the Senate and the House of Representatives more interdependent, and to abolish the possibilities of deadlocks between them, to make election to the Senate direct from the people, and to qualify and weaken the power of the two-party system by the introduction of "second ballots" and the referendum. . . .

But how such drastic changes are to be achieved constitutionally in America I cannot imagine. Only a great educated, trained, and sustained agitation can bring about so fundamental a political revolution, and at present I can find nowhere even the beginnings of a realization of this need.

V

President
Roosevelt
IN the White House, set midway between the Washington of the sight-seers and the Washington of brilliant conversation, I met President Roosevelt. I was

mightily pleased by the White House; it is dignified and simple—once again am I tempted to use the phrase "aristocratic in the best sense" of things American; and an entire absence of uniforms or liveries creates an atmosphere of Republican equality that is reinforced by "Mr. President's" friendly grasp of one's undistinguishable hand. And after lunch I walked about the grounds with him, and so achieved my ambition to get him "placed," as it were, in my vision of America.

In the rare chances I have had of meeting statesmen, there has always been one common effect, an effect of their being smaller, less audible, and less saliently featured than one had expected. A common man builds up his picture of the men prominent in the great game of life very largely out of caricature, out of head-lines, out of posed and "characteristic" portraits. One associates them with actresses and actors, literary poseurs and suchlike public performers, anticipates the same vivid self-consciousness as these display in common intercourse, keys one's self up for the paint on their faces, and for voices and manners altogether too accentuated for the gray-toned lives of common men. I've met politicians who remained at that. But so soon as Mr. Roosevelt entered the room, "Teddy," the Teddy of the slouch hat, the glasses, the teeth, and the sword, that strenuous vehement Teddy (who had, let me admit, survived a full course of reading in the President's earlier writings) vanished, and

gave place to an entirely negotiable individuality.
To-day, at any rate, the "Teddy" legend is untrue.
Perhaps it wasn't always quite untrue. There was
a time during the world predominance of Mr.
Kipling, when I think the caricature must have come
close to certain of Mr. Roosevelt's acceptances and
attitudes. But that was ten years and more ago,
and Mr. Roosevelt to this day goes on thinking and
changing and growing. . . .

For me, anyhow, that strenuousness has vanished
beyond recalling, and there has emerged a figure in
gray of a quite reasonable size, with a face far more
thoughtful and perplexed than strenuous, with a
clinched hand that does indeed gesticulate, though
it is by no means a gigantic fist—and with quick
movements, a voice strained indeed, a little forced
for oratory, but not raised or aggressive in any fashion, and friendly screwed-up eyes behind the glasses.

It isn't my purpose at all to report a conversation
that went from point to point. I wasn't interview-
ing the President, and I made no note at the time
of the things said. My impression was of a mind—
for the situation—quite extraordinarily open. That
is the value of President Roosevelt for me, and why
I can't for the life of my book leave him out. He
is the seeking mind of America displayed. The
ordinary politician goes through his career like a
charging bull, with his eyes shut to any changes in
the premises. He locks up his mind like a powder
magazine. But any spark may fire the mind of

President Roosevelt. His range of reading is amazing; he seems to be echoing with all the thought of the time, he has receptivity to the pitch of genius. And he does not merely receive, he digests and reconstructs; he thinks. It is his political misfortune that at times he thinks aloud. His mind is active with projects of solution for the teeming problems around him. Traditions have no hold upon him—nor, his enemies say, have any but quite formal pledges. It is hard to tie him. In all these things he is to a single completeness, to mind and will of contemporary America. And by an unparalleled conspiracy of political accidents, as all the world knows, he has got to the White House. He is not a part of the regular American political system at all—he has, it happens, stuck through.

Now my picture of America is, as I have tried to make clear, one of a gigantic process of growth, of economic coming and going, spaced out over vast distances and involving millions of hastening men; I see America as towns and urgency and greatnesses beyond, I suppose, any precedent that has ever been in the world. And like a little island of order amid that ocean of enormous opportunity and business turmoil and striving individualities, is this District of Columbia, with Washington and its Capitol and obelisk. It is a mere pin-point in the unlimited, on which, in peace times, the national government lies marooned, twisted up into knots, bound with safeguards, and altogether impotently stranded. And peering closely, and looking from the Capitol down the vista of Pennsylvania Avenue, I see the White House, minute and clear, with a fountain playing before it, and behind it a railed garden set with fine trees. The trees are not so thick, nor the railings so high but that the people on the big "seeing Washington" cannot crane to look into it and watch whoever walk about it. And in this garden goes a living speck, as it were, in gray, talking, swinging a white clinched hand, and trying vigorously and resolutely to get a hold upon the significance of the whole vast process in which he and his island of government are set.

Always before him there have been political resultants, irrelevancies and futilities of the White House; and after him, it would seem, they may come again. I do not know anything of the quality of Mr. Bryan, who may perhaps succeed him. He, too, is something of an exception, it seems, and keeps a still developing and inquiring mind. Beyond is a vista of figures of questionable value so far as I am concerned. They have this in common that they don't stand for thought. For the present, at any rate, a personality, extraordinarily representative, occupies the White House. And what he chooses to say publicly (and some things he says privately) are, by an exceptional law of acoustics, heard in San Francisco, in Chicago, in New Orleans, in New York and Boston, in Kansas, and Maine, throughout the whole breadth of the United States of America. He assimilates contemporary thought, delocalizes and reverberates it. He is America for the first time vocal to itself.

What is America saying to itself?

I've read most of the President's recent speeches, and they fall in oddly with that quality in his face that so many photographs even convey, a complex mingling of will and a critical perplexity. Taken all together they amount to a mass of not always consistent suggestions, that and conflict overlap. Things crowd upon him, rebate scandals, insurance scandals, the meat scandals, this insecurity and that. The conditions of his position press upon him. It is no wonder he gives out' no single, simple note. . . .

The plain fact is that in the face of the teeming situations of to-day America does not know what to do. Nobody, except those happily gifted individuals who can see but one aspect of an intricate infinitude, imagines any simple solution. For the rest the time is one of ample, vigorous, and at times impatient inquiry, and of intense disillusionment with old assumptions and methods. And never did a President before so reflect the quality of his time. The trend is altogether away from the anarchistic individualism of the nineteenth century, that much is sure, and towards some constructive scheme which, if not exactly socialism, as socialism is defined, will be, at any rate, closely analogous to socialism. This is the immense change of thought and attitude in which President Roosevelt participates, and to which he gives a unique expression. Day by day he changes with the big world about him — contradicts himself. . . .

I came away with the clear impression that neither President Roosevelt nor America will ever, as some people prophesy, "declare for socialism," but my impression is equally clear, that he and all the world of men he stands for, have done forever with the threadbare formulæ that have served America such an unconscionable time. We talked of the press and books and of the question of color, and then for a while about the rôle of the universities in the life of the coming time.

Now it is a curious thing that as I talked with President Roosevelt in the garden of the White House there came back to me quite forcibly that undertone of doubt that has haunted me throughout this journey. After all, does this magnificent appearance of beginnings which is America, convey any clear and certain promise of permanence and fulfilment whatever? Much makes for construction, a great wave of reform is going on, but will it drive on to anything more than a breaking impact upon even more gigantic uncertainties and dangers. Is America a giant childhood or a gigantic futility, a mere latest phase of that long succession of experiments which has been and may be for interminable years—may be indeed altogether until the end—man's social history? I can't now recall how our discursive talk settled towards that, but it is clear to me that I

struck upon a familiar vein of thought in the President's mind. He hadn't, he said, an effectual dis-
proof of any pessimistic interpretation of the future.
If one chose to say America must presently lose the
impetus of her ascent, that she and all mankind
must culminate and pass, he could not conclusively
deny that possibility. Only he chose to live as if
this were not so.

That remained in his mind. Presently he reverted
to it. He made a sort of apology for his life against
the doubts and scepticisms that, I fear, must be in
the background of the thoughts of every modern
man who is intellectually alive. He mentioned a
little book of mine, an early book full of the deliberate
pessimism of youth, in which I drew a picture of a
future of decadence, of a time when constructive
effort had fought its fight and failed, when the inevitable segregations of an individualistic system had
worked themselves out and all the hope and vigor of
humanity had gone forever. The descendants of the
workers had become etiolated, sinister, and sub-
terranean monsters, the property-owners had de-
generated into a hectic and feebly self-indulgent race,
living fitfully amid the ruins of the present time.
He became gesticulatory, and his straining voice a
note higher in denying this as a credible interpretation of destiny. With one of those sudden movements of his, he knelt forward in a garden chair—
we were standing before our parting beneath the
colonnade—and addressed me very earnestly over

the back, clutching it, and then thrusting out his familiar gesture, a hand first partly open and then closed.

"Suppose after all," he said, slowly, "that should prove to be right, and it all ends in your butterflies and morlocks. *That doesn't matter now.* The effort's real. It's worth going on with. It's worth it. It's worth it—even then." . . .

I can see him now and hear his unmusical voice saying "The effort—the effort's worth it," and see the gesture of his clinched hand and the—how can I describe it? the friendly peering snarl of his face, like a man with the sun in his eyes. He sticks in my mind as that, as a very symbol of the creative will in man, in its limitations, its doubtful adequacy, its valiant persistence amid perplexities and confusions. He kneels out, assertive against his setting—and his setting is the White House with a background of all America.

I could almost write, with a background of all the world—for I know of no other a tithe so representative of the creative purpose, the *good-will* in men as he. In his undisciplined hastiness, his limitations, his prejudices, his unfairness, his frequent errors, just as much as in his force, his sustained courage, his integrity, his open intelligence, he stands for his people and his kind.

THE ENVOY

AND at last I am back in my study by the sea. It is high June. When I said good-bye to things it was March, a March warm and eager to begin with, and then dashed with sleet and wind; but the daffodils were out, and the primulas and primroses shone brown and yellow in the unseasonable snow. The spring display that was just beginning is over. The iris rules. Outside the window is a long level line of black fleur-de-lys rising from a serried rank of leaf-blades. Their silhouettes stand out against the brightness of the twilight sea. They mark, so opened, two months of absence. And in the interval I have seen a great world.

I have tried to render it as I saw it. I have tried to present the first exhilaration produced by the sheer growth of it, the morning-time hopefulness of spacious and magnificent opportunity, the optimism of successful, swift, progressive effort in material things. And from that I have passed to my sense of the chaotic condition of the American will, and that first confidence has darkened more and more towards doubt again. I came to America questioning the certitudes of progress. For a time I forgot my questionings; I sincerely believed, "These people can do anything," and, now I have it all in perspective, I have to confess that doubt has taken me again. "These people," I say, "might do anything. They are the finest people upon earth—the most hopeful. But they are vain and hasty; they are thoughtless, harsh, and undisciplined. In the end, it may be, they will accomplish nothing." I see, I have noted in its place, the great forces of construction, the buoyant, creative spirit of America. But I have marked, too, the intricacy of snares and obstacles in its path. The problem of America, save in its scale and freedom, is no different from the problem of Great Britain, of Europe, of all humanity; it is one chiefly moral and intellectual; it is to resolve a confusion of purposes, traditions, habits, into a common ordered intention. Everywhere one finds what seem to me the beginnings of that—and, for this epoch it is all too possible, they may get no further than beginnings. Yet another Decline and Fall may remain to be written, another and another, and it may be another, before the World State comes and Peace.

Yet against this prospect of a dispersal of will, of a secular decline in honor, education, public spirit, and confidence, of a secular intensification of corruption, lawlessness, and disorder, I do, with a confidence that waxes and wanes, balance the creative spirit in America, and that kindred spirit that for me finds its best symbol in the President's kneeling, gesticulating figure, and his urgent "The effort's worth it!" Who can gauge the far-reaching influence of even the science we have, in ordering and quickening the imagination of man, in enhancing and assuring their powers? Common men feel secure to-day in enterprises it needed men of genius to conceive in former times. And there is a literature —for all our faults we do write more widely, deeply, disinterestedly, more freely and frankly than any set of writers ever did before—reaching incalculable masses of readers, and embodying an amount of common consciousness and purpose beyond all precedent. Consider only how nowadays the problems that were once the inaccessible thoughts of statesmen may be envisaged by common men! Here am I really able, in a few weeks of observant work, to get a picture of America. I publish it. If it bears a likeness, it will live and be of use; if not it will die, and be no irreparable loss. Some fragment, some suggestion may survive. My friend Mr. F. Madox Hueffer was here a day or so ago to say good-bye; he starts for America as I write here, to get *his* vision. As I have been writing these papers I have also been reading, instalment by instalment, the subtle, fine renderings of America revisited by Mr. Henry James. We work in shoals, great and small together, one trial thought following another. We are getting the world presented. It is not simply America that we swarm over and build up into a conceivable process, into something under-

standable and negotiable by the mind. I find on
my desk here waiting for me a most illuminating
Vision of India, in which Mr. Sidney Low, with a
marvellous aptitude, has interpreted east to west.
Besides my poor superficialities in *The Tribune* appears Sir William Butler, with a livid frankness expounding the most intimate aspects of the South
African situation. A friend who called to-day spoke
of Nevinson's raid upon the slave trade of Portuguese
East Africa, and of two irrepressible writers upon
the Congo crimes. I have already mentioned the
economic and social literature, the so-called literature
of exposure in America. This altogether represents
collectively a tremendous illumination. No social
development was ever so lit and seen before. Collectively, this literature of facts and theories and
impressions is of immense importance. Things are
done in the light, more and more are they done in the
light. The world perceives and thinks. . . .

After all is said and done, I do find the balance of
my mind tilts steadily to a belief in a continuing and
accelerated progress now in human affairs. And in
spite of my patriotic inclinations, in spite, too, of the
present high intelligence and efficiency of Germany,
it seems to me that in America, by sheer virtue of its
size, its free traditions, and the habit of initiative
in its people, the leadership of progress must ultimately rest. Things like the Chicago scandals, the insurance scandals, and all the manifest crudities of the
American spectacle, don't seem to me to be more

than relatively trivial after all. There are the universities, the turbines of Niagara, the New York architecture, and the quality of the mediocre people to set against these. . . .

Within a week after I saw the President I was on the *Umbria* and steaming slowly through the long spectacle of that harbor which was my first impression of America, which still, to my imagination, stands so largely for America. The crowded ferryboats hooted past; athwart the shining water, tugs clamored to and fro. The skyscrapers raised their slender masses heavenward—America's gay bunting lit the scene. As we dropped down I had a last glimpse of the Brooklyn Bridge. There to the right was Ellis Island, where the immigrants, minute by minute, drip and drip into America, and beyond that the tall spike-headed Liberty with the reluctant torch, which I have sought to make the centre of all this writing. And suddenly as I looked back at the skyscrapers of lower New York a queer fancy sprang into my head. They reminded me quite irresistibly of piled-up packing cases outside a warehouse. I was amazed I had not seen the resemblance before. I could really have believed for a moment that that was what they were, and that presently out of these would come the real thing, palaces and noble places, free, high circumstances, and space and leisure, light and fine living for the sons of men. . . .

Ocean, cities, multitudes, long journeys, mountains, lakes as large as seas, and the riddle of a nation's destiny; I've done my impertinent best now with this monstrous insoluble problem. I finish.

The air is very warm and pleasant in my garden to-night, the sunset has left a rim of greenish-gold about the northward sky, shading up a blue that is, as yet, scarce pierced by any star. I write down these last words here, and then I shall step through the window and sit out there in the kindly twilight, now quiet, now gossiping idly of what so-and-so has done while I have been away, of personal motives and of little incidents and entertaining intimate things.

THE END

Foreign Travelers in America
1810–1935

AN ARNO PRESS COLLECTION

Archer, William. **America To-Day**: Observations and Reflections. 1899.

Belloc, Hilaire. **The Contrast.** 1924.

[Boardman, James]. **America, and the Americans.** By a Citizen of the World. 1833.

Bose, Sudhindra. **Fifteen Years in America.** 1920.

Bretherton, C. H. **Midas, Or, The United States and the Future.** 1926.

Bridge, James Howard (Harold Brydges). **Uncle Sam at Home.** 1888.

Brown, Elijah (Alan Raleigh). **The Real America.** 1913.

Combe, George. **Notes on the United States Of North America During a Phrenological Visit in 1838-9-40.** 1841. 2 volumes in one.

D'Estournelles de Constant, Paul H. B. **America and Her Problems.** 1915.

Duhamel, Georges. **America the Menace**: Scenes from the Life of the Future. Translated by Charles Miner Thompson. 1931.

Feiler, Arthur. **America Seen Through German Eyes.** Translated by Margaret Leland Goldsmith. 1928.

Fidler, Isaac. **Observations on Professions, Literature, Manners, and Emigration, in the United States and Canada, Made During a Residence There in 1832.** 1833.

Fitzgerald, William G. (Ignatius Phayre). **Can America Last?** A Survey of the Emigrant Empire from the Wilderness to World-Power Together With Its Claim to "Sovereignty" in the Western Hemisphere from Pole to Pole. 1933.

Gibbs, Philip. **People of Destiny**: Americans As I Saw Them at Home and Abroad. 1920.

Graham, Stephen. **With Poor Immigrants to America.** 1914.

Griffin, Lepel Henry. **The Great Republic.** 1884.

Hall, Basil. **Travels in North America in the Years 1827 and 1828.** 1829. 3 volumes in one.

Hannay, James Owen (George A. Birmingham). **From Dublin to Chicago**: Some Notes on a Tour in America. 1914.

Hardy, Mary (McDowell) Duffus. **Through Cities and Prairie Lands:** Sketches of an American Tour. 1881.

Holmes, Isaac. **An Account of the United States of America,** Derived from Actual Observation, During a Residence of Four Years in That République, Including Original Communications. [1823].

Ilf, Ilya and Eugene Petrov. **Little Golden America:** Two Famous Soviet Humorists Survey These United States. Translated by Charles Malamuth. 1937.

Kerr, Lennox. **Back Door Guest.** 1930.

Kipling, Rudyard. **American Notes.** 1899.

Leng, John. **America in 1876:** Pencillings During a Tour in the Centennial Year, With a Chapter on the Aspects of American Life. 1877.

Longworth, Maria Theresa (Yelverton). **Teresina in America.** 1875. 2 volumes in one.

Low, A[lfred] Maurice. **America at Home.** [1908].

Marshall, W[alter] G[ore]. **Through America:** Or, Nine Months in the United States. 1881.

Mitchell, Ronald Elwy. **America:** A Practical Handbook. 1935.

Moehring, Eugene P. **Urban America and the Foreign Traveler, 1815-1855.** With Selected Documents on 19th-Century American Cities. 1974.

Muir, Ramsay. **America the Golden:** An Englishman's Notes and Comparisons. 1927.

Price, M[organ] Philips. **America After Sixty Years:** The Travel Diaries of Two Generations of Englishmen. 1936.

Sala, George Augustus. **America Revisited:** From the Bay of New York to the Gulf of Mexico and from Lake Michigan to the Pacific. 1883. 3rd edition. 2 volumes in one.

Saunders, William. **Through the Light Continent;** Or, the United States in 1877-8. 1879. 2nd edition.

Smith, Frederick [Edwin] (Lord Birkenhead). **My American Visit.** 1918.

Stuart, James. **Three Years in North America.** 1833. 2 volumes in one.

Teeling, William. **American Stew.** 1933.

Vivian, H. Hussey. **Notes of a Tour in America from August 7th to November 17th, 1877.** 1878.

Wagner, Charles. **My Impressions of America.** Translated by Mary Louise Hendee. 1906.

Wells, H. G. **The Future in America:** A Search After Realities. 1906.